50c

Jewish
as a
Second
Language

EXPANDED 2ND EDITION

Jewish
as a
Second
Language

How to Worry,
How to Interrupt,
How to Say the
Opposite of
What You Mean

BY MOLLY KATZ

Illustrated by Jeff Moores

WORKMAN PUBLISHING • NEW YORK

Copyright © 1999, 2010 by Molly Katz

Illustrations copyright © 2010 by Jeff Moores

All rights reserved. No portion of this book may be reproduced—
mechanically, electronically, or by any other means, including
photocopying—without written permission of the publisher.
Published simultaneously in Canada by Thomas Allen & Son Limited.

Library of Congress Cataloging-in-Publication Data is available.

ISBN 978-0-7611-5840-0

Design by Yin Ling Wong

Workman books are available at special discounts when purchased in
bulk for premiums and sales promotions as well as for fund-raising or
educational use. Special editions or book excerpts can also be created
to specification. For details, contact the Special Sales Director at the
address below or send an e-mail to specialsales@workman.com.

Workman Publishing Company, Inc.
225 Varick Street
New York, NY 10014-4381
www.workman.com

Printed in the United States of America

First printing March 2010

10 9 8 7 6 5 4 3 2 1

DEDICATION

My heartfelt thanks to Henry Morrison, Kylie Foxx McDonald, Peter Workman, Susan Bolotin, Jeff Moores, Yin Ling Wong, Irene Demchyshyn, and Kevin McDonald. It's a joy to work and laugh with you. Somewhere Sally Kovalchick is laughing with us. Thanks also to Bill Parkhurst for the unending inspiration, and the willingness to not only take a joke, but enthusiastically contribute many.

ACKNOWLEDGMENTS

These great people joined in the fun: Steve Simon, Toba Simon, Peg Chivers, Terry Katz, Chris Katz, Julie Ross, Sherry Koski, Tom Koski, Peggy Haering, William Singer, Lavonne Woodworth, Carolyn Parkhurst, Evan Rosser, Ellie Grossman, Carol Guernsey, Patricia Mack Newton, Mark Adams, Bill Shortell, Helene Morrison, Dr. Esme Singer, Candace Carlisle, Dick Akin (of Dick and the Dickettes), Eleanor Craig Green, Paul Green, Nancy Hannah, Sarah Durand, Peggy Crane, Paul Crane, June Hurtgen, Dr. Doreen Parkhurst, Marge Garfield, Maureen Sherman, Jerry Sherman, Andre Louw, Janet Pollack, Mary Kenney, Karen Santopietro, Dr. Keith Rudolph, Len Tanner, Ruth Doan MacDougall, Don MacDougall, Mandy Muden, Merle Nacht, Bruce Morrison, Dr. Denis Sivak, Dr. Felice Zwas, Al Zullo, Diane "Killer" Miller

Contents

CHAPTER 4
Your New Jewish Body

CHAPTER 5
Building Your New Jewish Economic Perspective

CHAPTER 6
Raising Your Jewish Child

CHAPTER 7

Joining in the Customs of Your New Jewish Family

CHAPTER 8

Readiness Test

Introduction

I AM JEWISH. MY EX-HUSBAND BILL IS NOT. ONE DAY, BACK WHEN we were still married, my mother had to get her blood pressure checked. She didn't need a ride, she said; she'd call a cab. Bill said, "Okay."

Of course, she stopped speaking to us.

"How could you?" I asked Bill.

"How could I what?"

"Let her take a cab."

"But," Bill said, "it was her idea."

"You should have known how to translate," I said.

He said, "*My* mother would have taken a cab."

"She's not Jewish. If a Jewish person offers to take a cab, she never *means* it."

"Well, you'll have to be patient with me," he said. "Jewish is only my second language."

> **Not** your religion.
> ("She's Jewish, but her husband's Not.")

Thus the first edition of this book was born—to help Bill and other confused Nots decipher the intricate codes of Jewish communication. And now I'm back, by popular demand, with more help for the innocent, unsuspecting non-Jewish person marrying into a Jewish family (not that there's anything wrong with that). If this describes you, it means you've been chosen to join the ranks of the Chosen People, to which I say: *mazel tov*[1] and good luck (you're going to need it). Consider this book a handy field guide to your crazy new world and everything in it. If you're not the marrying type, you'll still find the book useful—especially if you plan to work with Jews, become a Jew, or if you're traveling to New York or Florida.

It's been years since the first *Jewish as a Second Language* came out, to great success—which means the generation I wrote it for has produced a fresh generation of lambs to the . . . I mean, young people considering this step. And recently, people began grumbling, saying they want more (that is, people where Jewish is spoken, which leaves out Iraq, Iran, Chad, and Hilton Head). I heard from all sorts of wayward souls, including current members of Jewish families, and also ex-members, pending members, and honorary members.[2]

"Mol," they begged, "why didn't you tell us about Jewish Ping-Pong? About the revolution in Jewish travel? About leaving maddening voicemail messages? You skipped over so much!"

---

[1] **Mazel tov:** Good luck, but with nuance. Jews speak this phrase with many meanings, from "I hope you succeed" to "I hope you fail like I did."

[2] **Honorary member:** A family associate or employee, such as a nanny or manicurist, who everyone in the family pretends is as good as they are.

I felt guilty, tormented by anxiety . . . *how many other things had I left out?* I wanted to help these people, but then again, maybe they were overreacting. So, I decided to mount a nationwide poll. I posed the following questions:

1. Are you planning to marry/work with a Jewish person?

> **Yes** 40%
>
> **No** 40%
>
> **Didn't We Do This Already?** 20%

2. If yes, do you feel comfortable with his/her family?

> **Yes** 0%
>
> **No** 77%
>
> **Just Stab Me Now** 23%

3. Need some help fitting in?

> **No** 11%
>
> **Yes** 43%
>
> **I Need to Breathe, Too, but That Can Wait** 46%

4. Do you think I should write an updated, expanded version of *Jewish as a Second Language?*

> **No** 0%
>
> **Yes** 20%
>
> **Absolutely, and I Think They Should Pay You a Lot More Money for It This Time** 80%

And the verdicts came in: The *goyim*[3] needed my assistance once again. Heeding their call, I dug deep to answer the difficult questions. I explored the great themes, like how far is *shofar*,[4] and what are the differences between *babka*[5] and *bupkes*.[6] I share my findings with you here, in these pages, offering further guidelines to your new Jewish family and the far-from-unlimited world around it. You'll find out about Vanilla Jews, Regular Jews, New Jews, Very Jewish Jews, and Even More Jewish Very Jewish Jews. You'll learn to brag and extort sympathy at the same time. You'll be taught to create brilliantly sneaky attack questions. You'll learn never to use that bacteria-laden sponge on my dishes ever again.

Once, nobody married Jews except other Jews (and rich, neurotic non-Jews trying to torture their Patrician families; this was usually done after alternate methods, such as piercing their petzel, schnitzel, and other nether parts, had failed). But there are many of you out there now, non-Jews swimming in the rubber cement of our mores, and you need help. There is much to learn about things you thought you already knew how to do, such as talk, think, eat, feel, and behave. Keeping a low profile, in the hope that observation and tact will help smooth the transition, is about as effective as politely introducing yourself to a scorpion.

To learn the Jewish language, you need to understand one point especially: This does not mean Yiddish, the Eastern European language derived from German with which we Jews often pepper

---

[3] **Goyim:** Gentiles. A word that's not supposed to be pejorative, but often is. ("I'll serve tiramisu and save the sponge cake for the *goyim*.")

[4] **Shofar:** A ceremonial ram's horn that, when sounded, damages your eardrums no matter how far away you are.

[5] **Babka:** A delicious, fattening cake.

[6] **Bupkes:** Nothing. ("Have some *babka*! It's got no calories, *bupkes*.")

our English. You'll never have to speak Yiddish, except to stumble over a word or phrase occasionally with the awkwardness expected of you. (Jews know you're uncomfortable with Yiddish. We know you feel left out. As well you should: It's designed to *keep* you out.)

We like to believe your tongue can't form the tangles of consonants necessary to say a Yiddish word. Therefore, no matter how it comes out, you'll be corrected. One of us will explain to you that *gonif,* the way you pronounced it, doesn't simply mean thief, but a Bosnian thief who steals your sister's ankle bracelet.

Don't try to polish your pronunciation, though. Instead, learn just enough Yiddish to make your errors truly hysterical. This effort will pay off in improved family relations: Your in-laws will have a blast hooting at your mistakes (which they know you'll find endearing).

Be sure your usage is faulty, too. This confirms our conviction that Yiddish defies translation, that mere English can't match its intricate layers of meaning— and that non-Jews are hopeless when they try to use it. We love to hear you deliver howlers like "When she found out she wasn't invited, she made such a big *schmatta,*[7] you could hear her down the street" or "Put everything on my bagel—nova, onions, the whole *schlemiel.*"[8]

---

[7] **Schmatta:** A rag. ("Oh, this? Just a *schmatta* I picked up at Dior.")

[8] **Schlemiel:** A poor fool. ("What a *schlemiel!* He thinks she bought that *schmatta* at T.J. Maxx.")

No, the true language of Jews is not Yiddish. It is the complex twists and somersaults of everyday conversation, the swamps and thickets of behavior. It is nuances and expectations, hidden meanings and unvoiced point systems . . . wins, losses, and draws in competitions you had no idea you'd entered.

This book is your guide to the mysterious web of your new environment. Study it carefully, and the secrets of our universe will unfold.

ON JOiNiNG A JEWiSH FAMiLY

DISADVANTAGES	ADVANTAGES
You'll never have a brother-in-law who can replace your voltage regulator.	You won't have to look at baseball caps on backwards.
You'll have to sell your bowling ball.	You'll never have to climb a ladder.
You can kiss caffeine good-bye.	You'll eat the best baked goods money can buy.
You'll have to scrape off all your hilarious bumper stickers (see page 173).	No one will give your child an ant farm.
No one in the family will get drunk with you when the Yankees win the pennant.	There will always be plenty of sweaters in the house. Any house. Even in Miami.

DISADVANTAGES	ADVANTAGES
No one in the family will get drunk with you when the Yankees lose the pennant.	You'll never have to live with indoor-outdoor carpeting, aluminum siding, or an aboveground pool.
No one in the family will get drunk with you.	Your in-laws will insist on believing your forebears settled Plymouth Rock, even if the only ancestor you know of was a hash-addicted hunchback from Flanders.

A TECHNIQUE TO LEARN RIGHT AWAY. THIS SECOND. BEFORE YOU EVEN EAT.

YOU'VE HEARD OF FAQS; WELL, FROM NOW ON, YOU MUST learn to ask Obsessive Anal Questions (OAQs). All Jews do this. It is our comfort and our oral *mezuzah*.[7] You'll see ideas for appropriate questions in each chapter; to qualify, they must be fussy, whiny, and impossible to address. It is the act of conceptualizing and voicing the question that lets God know you're aware of what He might have in store for some poor, unsuspecting

[7] **Mezuzah:** A piece of prayer parchment contained in a metal cylinder that is affixed to one's front door as a reminder of God's presence. OAQs are to remind God of our presence.

putz [10]—but it better not be you. This is how we beat God at His own game. When He knows we're on to His nefarious plans, they are rendered futile.

Soon you'll become adept at thinking up your own OAQs. With practice, you can even become one of the non-question non-answerers.

Some basics to get you started:

"Do I look all right?"

"What's that noise?"

"Is there enough?"

"This mole looks okay, doesn't it?"

"Do you smell anything?"

"What's going to happen?"

"They'll de-ice the wings before takeoff, right?"

"Do you hear that little wheeze when I breathe? Not on the inhale, but on the exhale. Listen . . ."

"Is it just me?"

---

[10] **Putz:** Literally, a penis. Used to describe a man you can't get away with calling a prick.

CHAPTER 1

Developing Jewish Conversational Skills

HOW TO IDENTIFY A GOOD CONVERSATION

FORGET THE CLICHÉS YOU'VE HEARD ABOUT JEWS' LOVE OF learning. What we love more than that is *talking,* so plan on doing a monumental amount of it. You'll be holding conversations with your in-laws, with friends of the family, with everyone *they* converse with. Here's how to make sure you know what you're doing.

✱ By now you've had at least twenty-odd years in which to finish your sentences. This is enough for anybody. We hope you enjoyed the luxury while you had it, because you'll never finish one again. Nor would you want to. The more interruptions, the more enthusiastic the conversation. Three or four people talking at once is ideal. This is your signal of acceptance. If no one jumps in to join the fun, it means that what you're saying is boring.

✱ Another indication that your new family enjoys conversing with you is when they ask lots of friendly questions. Things like "We heard your brother is a registered sex offender" and "Is it true your uncle was disbarred?" are signs that they're really taking an interest.

✱ You'll know you're a truly valued conversational partner when they do you the honor of sharing crucial points of advice. Observations such as "You look nauseating in teal" or "That haircut emphasizes your double chin" should erase any insecurity you may still have about your role as a companion in repartee.

WHERE TO CONVERSE

WHETHER WE'RE TALKING WITH FRIENDS, ACQUAINTANCES, clerks, or total strangers, the most enjoyable Jewish conversations are impromptu. They occur in the following locations:

At the Supermarket. When you run into a friend here, of course you must catch up. Select a narrow aisle piled with cartons. Position your shopping carts so no one can get by. Feel free to chat as long and as loudly as you wish. Ignore the glares of other shoppers—they're just jealous of the good time you're having.

In a Department Store. The salesclerk showing you a lipstick will be glad to wait while you catch up with the friend who's just greeted you. That's what the clerk's there for. Never be so rude as to exclude her from your talk. If your friend doesn't think to get the clerk's input on her upcoming hysterectomy, *you* do it.

In a Restaurant. If you see people you know, hurry to the table no matter where they are in their meal. They'll be eager to chat with you and introduce their tablemates. Make sure everyone joins the conversation. They can eat anytime.

At a Party. Ignore all the guests you don't know; they can talk to their *own* friends. Scream to familiar faces to come join you. Spend the entire evening trying to outyell one another on the most inconsequential topics. You'll know you're doing this correctly when the room rings with shouts like "What do you *mean* you haven't fertilized your lawn all summer?"

Through Your Bathroom Door. You'd better learn to pee fast, because from now on you have only thirty seconds before the family starts worrying. At that time someone will stand outside the door and yell, "Are you okay?" Touch up your mascara somewhere else, because you'll be questioned again and again as long as you're in there.

Meanwhile, those outside will be guessing what's taking you all this time. Trust me, mascara is not one of the guesses. When you come out, don't be surprised when asked, "Are you constipated? It runs in Barry's family, you know" or "Bleeding a lot? Aunt Darlene had that. It was uterine cancer."

On a Waiting Line. Jews love lines. Aside from the fact that finding one at the movie or other event we've picked confirms the brilliance of our choice, we consider a waiting line our personal studio audience.

As soon as you reach the line, ask the person in front of you if he or she is at the end. Ask as many other questions as you can think of, even if the person obviously knows no more than you do. When you're out of questions, begin talking to the person you came with. Keep up a running dialogue about everyone walking by and everything happening around you. Do this in a tone so loud that others on line know they're expected to join the conversation. With practice, you can hone this technique so exquisitely that bystanders feel guilty for keeping silent.

9 WAYS *NOT* TO START A CONVERSATION WITH A JEWISH PERSON

1. "How do you get rid of pinworms?"

2. "I put miniature marshmallows in my instant chocolate pudding."

3. "Is that real, or Diamonique?"

4. "A priest, a minister, and a rabbi were in a lifeboat . . ."

5. "Where can I get a deal on a snowblower?"

6. "Got a bus schedule on you?"

7. "I forgot to put this tuna salad in the refrigerator. It's still good, isn't it?"

8. "What's your favorite water park?"

9. "Them Bruins gonna win the Stanley Cup?"

CONVERSATIONAL STRATEGY

AN ESSENTIAL ELEMENT OF YOUR NEW COMMUNICATION skills is the ability to make statements that express the opposite of what you mean. This is generally done in two ways.

1. The Positive Insult. A comment that masquerades as a put-down but, properly translated, makes the other person feel good.

APPARENT INSULT	TRANSLATION
"This Queen Anne table is so pretentious."	"I wish I could afford it."
"Isn't your Jessica wearing too much blush?"	"Too bad my Hilary has a face like a waffle iron."
"That brocade suit is much too dressy for a brunch."	"I wish I could afford it."
"How can you eat this junk? It's loaded with fat."	"If I weren't twenty-five pounds overweight, I'd eat it, too."
"You're crazy to buy a Jag. They break down in the rain."	"I wish I could afford it."

nice; nic·er; nic·est An all-purpose, meaningless adjective *("I'm dying of thirst. Bring me a nice glass of water.")*

2. The Negative Compliment. The reverse of the positive insult; a candy-coated torpedo.

APPARENT COMPLIMENT	TRANSLATION
"How wonderful that you and Milton can get away so often."	"Some of us *work* for a living."
"What a fudge cake! You must have put in a pound of butter."	"I'm going to be up all night with diarrhea."
"Your husband is such a fabulous dancer."	"How come he married a klutz?"
"I love how your diamond reflects the light."	"Just *say* you're engaged to a cardiologist. You don't have to blind us."
"Your son is quite the artist!"	"So you WANT him still living home in 20 years?"

JEWISH PHRASEOLOGY

AVERAGE, HUMDRUM THINGS NEVER HAPPEN TO JEWS. Even the weather isn't the same for us as it is for others, regardless of the fact that it's the same weather. Accordingly, all our expressions are maximums, superlatives, and extremes.

YOU USED TO:	BUT NOW YOU:
Get caught in the rain	Get drenched in a downpour
Have a headache	Have a terrible headache
Be tired	Are totally exhausted
Taste something good	Have discovered something absolutely out of this world
Be warm or cold	Are boiling or freezing
Say a road was slippery	Say it's a sheet of ice
Be hungry	Are starving to death
Be surprised	Have cardiac arrest
Feel anxious	Are shaking like a leaf
Be allergic	Are violently allergic

ACRONYMS

God, how we love using these when we talk. It makes us seem in-the-know to say, "They rushed Louie to the hospital for an emergency upper GI" or "My niece Brandi got a job at P & G."

There are, however, some acronyms that, as a Jew, you won't be using:

ATV: *All-Terrain Vehicle* Jews don't use this term; to us there's only one type of vehicle, and it has individual climate control for each passenger.

ROTC: *Reserve Officers' Training Corps* Some military *mishegoss*[1] non-Jews do in college.

STD: *Sexually Transmitted Disease* "Cheryl's daughter got an STD at Oberlin. She should have gone to Brandeis."

NASCAR: *National Association for Stock Car Auto Racing* Smashups, grease, and terrible refreshments. Oy.

TRO: *Temporary Restraining Order* For non-Jews who can't yell loud enough and need a judge to make someone stop bothering them.

DIY: *Do-It-Yourself (as a project, like digging a well)* Um, what?

DOA: *Dead on Arrival* No Jews ever say this, except possibly lawyers.

MRSA (pronounced *mur-sa*): *Methicillin-resistant Staphylococcus aureus* A potentially deadly skin infection spread by contact, and also by talking about it casually.

[1] **Mishegoss:** Craziness.

BODY LANGUAGE

YOU UNDOUBTEDLY WATCH IN AWE AS YOUR NEW RELATIVES converse among themselves, using not just their voices but as many body parts as are humanly movable. To join in, you'll need to master these communication skills.

THE SHRUGS

A shrug is achieved by lifting the shoulders. It may be accompanied by your choice of faces and hand movements (see facing page). The intensity of the shrugged emotion is indicated by the degree to which the neck is hidden. When practicing shrugs, be sure to wear a little sweater (see page 20) to ward off muscle spasms.

The Four Basic Shrugs

✻ **Incredulous** ("I was supposed to know it would rain?")

✻ **Helpless** ("Me? Lift *that*?")

✻ **Stymied** ("Google it.")

✻ **All-purpose** ("Go know.")

THE FACES

✳ **Pained** ("That's the best you can do?")

✳ **Bug-eyed** (*"How* much?")

✳ **Aggrieved** ("No letter, no call, nothing.")

✳ **Dissatisfied** ("I said paint it *light* sunburst, not dark.")

✳ **Shocked** ("Rejected? *Me*?")

✳ **Pleased** ("I told you that chair would break if you stood on it.")

THE HANDS

✳ **Waving** ("Doctor, schmoctor. He's an *optometrist.*")

✳ **Raised, palms out** ("Stop *yelling.*")

✳ **Extended** ("Would I lie?")

✳ **On head** (*"Now* what?")

✳ **Applauding** ("You finally got it right.")

UNDERSTANDING JEWISH CHITCHAT

TO FULLY APPRECIATE CONVERSING WITH YOUR NEW FAMILY, you will need to learn our unique Jewish expressions and familiarize yourself with some eccentric usage.

BASIC VOCABULARY

Crime A little bit of a shame ("It's a crime to waste these nectarines.")

Little sweater A cardigan. For no known reason, it is never called just a sweater. It has curative and protective powers. ("I'm freezing in here. Get me a little sweater." Or, "Take a little sweater so you don't catch a chill.")

IfGodforbid An advance antidote. Since God monitors everything Jews say, it's vital not to give Him any ideas. You must signal Him so He'll know what you *don't* want ("IfGodforbid Sol should lose one of his stores . . .")

nausea A state of being that has nothing to do with the stomach. ("I tried Neiman's. Their resortwear collection is nauseating." Or, "We had to let the Benz go for forty-five-five. We were nauseous.")

THE BAKERY RAN OUT OF ONION RYE. IT'S A CRIME.

feh An expression of indifference, often used to communicate that you are not impressed, especially when you are:

BRENDA: "My Debbie was accepted at Yale, Dartmouth, and Harvard."

THERESA: "Congratulations."

JANET: "Feh."

ODDiTiES OF USAGE

You must tune your ear to some new verbal twists. The present tense, for example, is used to express the passage of time. The answer to "How long are you married?" is not "Until death do us part" but "Three years." The answer to "How long do you have this roof leak?" is "Since I'm living here."

Other peculiarities include:

1. The contraction, preceded by "so" and accompanied by a shrug, used to express the obvious solution to a problem:

✱ "What if we can't get a reservation at the Ritz?" "*So* we'll stay at the Four Seasons."

✱ "My car is in the shop." "*So* you'll rent one."

Dear Ms. Jewish,
What is the difference between "nu" and "new?"

Dear Ms. Not,
Here is the difference:
New: not old.
Nu: serves as a variety of questions:
So? Well? What?

Thus:
"Isaac bought a car."
"Nu, is it new?"

2. **The verb,** a part of speech with which their sentences Jews often end:

  ✴ "If he runs out of money, so he'll call and you'll send."

  ✴ "There's cheesecake left. Who doesn't have?"
  "I don't have."
  "So come over here and get."

3. **What,** used with the emphasis on the second word, to underscore the ludicrousness of a notion:

  ✴ "We'll give Jason Google stock for graduation."
  "What *stock*? We'll give him a Lexus."

  ✴ "I heard your sister bought a beach cottage."
  "What *cottage*? It's a tri-level converted duck barn with six and a half baths."

One More Thing You'll Never Hear a Jewish Person Say

"No Problem."

Because:
1. There is no such thing as a situation that is not a problem, and
2. No Jewish person would suggest a favor isn't being done when one is.

14 THINGS YOU WON'T HEAR A JEWISH PERSON SAY

1. "Yeah, my kid will never amount to much, either."

2. "Less is more."

3. "No, thanks, I don't eat between meals."

4. "Ch-Ch-Ch-Chia!"

5. "Let me show you around the trailer park."

6. "It just *happened.*"

7. "A lawyer? Sorry, I don't know any."

8. "There's a new calf in the barn."

9. "Love is blind."

10. "I forgot to make hotel reservations. Oh, well—we'll camp out."

11. "Sorry to bother you."

12. "Got a light?"

13. "You're not hungry, are you?"

14. "Here, pooch, snuggle up with us. Oops. Put flea spray on the grocery list."

WHAT NOT TO DISCUSS

I N YOUR NEW JEWISH FAMILY, CONVERSATIONAL TABOOS HAVE nothing to do with taste (a concept as foreign to your new relatives as Rocky Mountain Oysters) and everything to do with fear.

It's perfectly fine to describe the details of your bleeding ulcer, or the terrible intestinal virus you picked up in Nevis. But certain words must always be said in a whisper, to prevent them from being attracted to you. These include:

Tumor

Parasite

Biopsy

Fatal

Embolism

Wart

Malignancy

Sexually Transm . . .

A quick and easy way to remember the principle is this:

DISGUSTING = DISCUSSABLE

You can talk about anything that went into or came out of a living body (not even necessarily human—my friend Candace married into a family where her mother-in-law bought scented wipettes at Saks to clean the dog's *tochas*[2] after each walk).

---

[2] **Tochas:** Oh, *you know.*

You can't discuss *dead* bodies for the same reason you can't mention cancer—God is in charge of these, and He might get the wrong idea. But if the market is plunging, talk about that all you want. Even God fears the Dow.

Let's say Arlene is in the hospital with a mysterious eye infection. You visit her.

DO: No matter how gross or contagious the oozing eye looks, lean in very close and examine it. If others are with you, everyone should bend down together to peer at it (thus ensuring that anything you don't catch from the patient you'll get from somebody else). Thoroughly discuss the color and viscosity of the pus and any other detritus. It's fine to make faces or retching noises.

DON'T: Ask if there's a Lump, a Spot, or a Growth.

Now imagine Uncle Gary comes over to play Texas Hold 'em and he can't sit down because of his hemorrhoids.

DO: Talk about your own hemorrhoids, and those of anyone else you've ever met. Tell him what remedies to try, especially the ones that are really vile to administer.

DON'T: Ask meaningfully, "When was your last colonoscopy?"

THE SiNGLE-WORD SALVO

THE OBJECT OF THIS TECHNIQUE IS TO CRAM AS MUCH recrimination into as few words as possible. When intoned correctly, even a syllable or two can

✴ Leave the questioner consumed with remorse because they should have shown more interest, earlier, or with appropriately dramatic concern—

"How are you feeling?"
"Better."

. . . and . . .

"What time did your daughter get here?"
"Late."

—while at the same time punishing the questioner by depriving them of the whole story.

✴ Communicate your wish to be included when you wouldn't dream of rudely inviting yourself. For instance, three women are chatting:

RUTH: "Helene, what are you and Henry doing for New Year's?"
HELENE: "We're going to the Delano. How about you?"
RUTH: "Fred and I are having caviar and Chateaubriand at
home. Sharon, what are you and Marc doing?"
SHARON: "Nothing."

✱ Remind the person of your expected timetable:

"I called the landscaper."
"Finally."

✱ Let slip a hint of your feelings about a new family member:

"We loved the wedding. Where are your daughter
and Angus living?"
"Who?"

Single words are also an effective frame in which to nag
or criticize:

She's just started dressing to go out: "Ready?"

He claims he left the bathroom clean: "Really?"

She just ate four brownies: "Enough?"

He calls from the golf course: "Finished?"

She yawns after sleeping late: "Tired?"

He's relaxing on the sofa: "Comfy?"

PRESSURE

NEARLY ANY BANAL INTERACTION, IF YOU RESPOND IN THE right way, can be twisted around to make you the victim and the other person the wrongdoer. When done properly, these techniques will cause the other person to feel guilt, frustration, anxiety, and an intense compulsion to make the situation better, or, at the very least, kowtow to you.

APPLYiNG PRESSURE

Someone comes late: "I was so worried."

Someone cancels: "We were all looking forward to seeing you."

Someone doesn't call you back: "I was sure something happened."

Someone lets herself into your house: "The bell is broken?"

BEiNG PRESSURED

Someone e-mails you and says, "I understand you have a wonderful dog groomer you adore": They're looking for a recommendation, of course, but more important, they're telegraphing who will be to blame if they don't adore the groomer, too.

Someone calls your cell while you're in a restaurant and says, irritatedly, "You can't possibly hear me with all that noise": They're annoyed at having to talk to you where *you* are. How quickly they forget who called whom. They expect you to go home right away so they can talk to you in peace and quiet.

BONDiNG

I T'S YOUR CULTURAL RESPONSIBILITY TO IDENTIFY YOURSELF to any person you think might be Jewish. As soon as you learn someone's name is Horowitz or Zilkenstein, say something friendly like, "Oy! Another member of the tribe!" Then go on to insert Yiddish words[3] into your conversation. This is especially welcome in a business setting ("So you're in granite? Do you know Kipferberg, the *schmendrick*, the *momser*?").

If you still don't get a return fusillade of warmth, say, "I knew you'd understand, since your name is Rosenbergwitz. Go tell Kipferberg it's a *shandeh*, the *gelt* he owes me."

Don't give up if your friendliness isn't immediately reciprocated. Keep at it. You know that under his pretend WASP exterior, there's a Jewish heart beating in his chest.

---

[3] **Gelt:** Money.

Schmendrick: An idiot. ("What a schmendrick! He lost all his gelt.")

Momser: A bastard. ("What a momser! He stole that schmendrick's gelt.")

Shandeh: A shame. ("Such a shandeh the schmendrick has no gelt for a lawyer to sue that momser.")

TELLING PEOPLE WHAT THEY SHOULD AND SHOULDN'T HAVE DONE

WHAT PEOPLE SHOULD OR SHOULDN'T HAVE DONE ARE interchangeable—because the point of saying either is for you to be right, and for the other person, regardless of his or her actions, to be wrong.

YOU: "You drove into the city? Which way did you go?"
OTHER PERSON: "The bridge."
YOU: "Never. You should have taken the tunnel."

OR

YOU: "You drove into the city? Which way did you go?"
OTHER PERSON: "The tunnel."
YOU: "Bad call. The bridge is always better."

The object here is, of course, to entertain yourself. But the more truly Jewish you become, the more you will actually believe every word you're saying.

TELEPHONE CONVERSATION

FEW ACCESSORIES ARE AS VITAL TO JEWISH LIFE AS THE telephone. This auditory pacemaker has its own set of etiquette rules.

1. When making a call, converse with someone near you as you dial. Be in the middle of a sentence as your party answers. Complete the sentence before greeting your party.

Repeat the procedure when answering the phone. When this is done properly, the caller will hear a greeting such as "—hate playing tennis when I have my period. Hello?"

2. Remember, it's rude to talk on the phone with nothing in your mouth. Always have something crunchy, like a toasted English muffin, on hand in case the phone rings. Take large bites and chew audibly, pausing only when the other person is speaking.

3. Have frequent side conversations. Scream at someone several rooms away without moving your mouth from the receiver.

4. Put your caller on hold as often as possible. Do you want people to think no one else calls you?

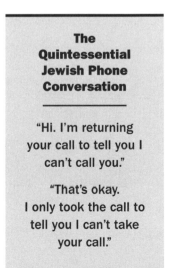

The Quintessential Jewish Phone Conversation

"Hi. I'm returning your call to tell you I can't call you."

"That's okay. I only took the call to tell you I can't take your call."

TELEPHONE COACHING (JEWISH JUMPING JACKS)

It takes at least three Jews to have a phone conversation. There are two ways to do this:

1. Put the call on speakerphone. The parties at both ends will all talk at once and nobody will hear anything, which is okay, because Jews always talk and never listen—and because whatever is being discussed will be talked to death over and over again anyway.

2. One or both sides will have an extra participant. It is this person's job to pester the person holding the phone about what to say—and to keep asking him or her to repeat what the other person said. When this is done correctly, the third participant will be shushed repeatedly and end up jumping around in frustration (which is good, because it's the only exercise he or she ever gets).

WHAT TO SAY WHEN YOU HEAR AN OFF NOTE

Situation

You're on the phone with a friend. You suspect she's not giving the conversation her full cheerful attention.

Pre-Jewish Reaction. Not wishing to pry, you say nothing about it.

New Reaction. Ask accusingly, "Are you upset? Are you irritated? You don't sound right." To any explanation offered, say dubiously, "Uh huh." Corkscrew in on finding the reason. Make it clear through your tone and strategic pauses that you're taking this personally.

With practice, you can get the other person practically singing and dancing to make up for whatever insult she never made anyway.

VOICEMAIL

No Jew ever declines an opportunity to have their words recorded. However, this is different when a human isn't doing the recording, and therefore isn't present to appreciate your impressive vocabulary and perfect diction. What fun is it to talk into a silent nothing?

✱ As a Jewish person, you will now hate calling someone and getting their voicemail. How dare a stupid machine waste your time? You'll be tempted to hang up. But why squander a perfectly good opportunity to punish the person for not answering the phone? At least make a disgusted noise before you hang up.

Or, to make sure your call is returned immediately, leave a message such as, "It's Martha. *Don't worry.*"

✳ Jews know that robbers, rapists, and homicidal maniacs spend their time randomly dialing numbers, hoping to find an empty house where they can steal everything, or lie in wait to victimize the returning owner. Therefore your outgoing voicemail message should say something like, "We're home, but we're unable to come to the phone. Leave a message and one of us, probably our son the District Attorney, will call you back." This ensures that the criminal will immediately reject you and instead go stab some poor schmuck who's too unsophisticated to protect himself.

CONVERSATION OAQs

"Why does Roberta have to talk so loud
and break my eardrums?"

"Doesn't Herman ever shut up?"

"Why isn't Deirdre calling me back?
Is something wrong?"

"Did you hear the tone of her voice?"

CHAPTER 2

The Jewish Home

INTERIOR DECORATION

NOW THAT YOU HAVE A JEWISH HOME, YOU MUST MAKE SURE it looks like one, i.e., like everyone else's in the family. Jews get insecure in unfamiliar settings. To ensure your relatives' comfort, and establish the appropriate surroundings for your new lifestyle, make certain your home conforms, visually and functionally, in these essential ways.

Broadloom. A generic word for floor covering, the purpose of which is to keep you worrying about preventing dents in the pile. Furniture legs never rest on it, but on plastic circles. So that the circles won't make dents, they sit on nice little squares of broadloom atop the actual broadloom. While broadloom may be used in most any room, it is always found in the . . .

Living Room. This must include fragile furniture, paintings, and a grand piano. The piano is for displaying family pictures. It is never played. IfGodforbid someone tries to play it, they'll be told, "There are people downstairs." (This is the case even if you're in a ranch house.) The paintings often have viewing lights, which are never turned on. Since the room isn't entered except to be cleaned, no living is done here. It is done in the . . .

Family Room. An area whose focus derives from that favorite Jewish activity, **sitting.** All furniture is chosen and upholstered in terms of how good it is for **sitting.** The floor covering must be comfortable to **sit** on. The TV and stereo are positioned according to where those using them will **sit.** The family room is a vital part of your house, but definitely secondary to the . . .

Bathroom. The heart of the Jewish home. It is here that one is cleaned, inside and out, and this room must be decorated and supplied in line with the importance of what takes place within its walls. Spare no expense acquiring the thickest towels, the softest toilet paper.

A new family member who is truly committed to Jewish life must become completely self-absorbed in the performance of bathroom functions. You'll know you've mastered this when you find yourself discussing toilet habits and gastrointestinal events as avidly as if they were terrorism bulletins.

DECORATiNG GUiDELiNES

✳ Never use a decorator. If you do, say you didn't.

✳ Choose impractical pale colors and whisper-thin fabrics for your living room. This enables you to hover and fret whenever someone is in danger of sitting on the furniture or walking on the broadloom.

✳ Order floor-to-ceiling draperies for the living room and bedrooms. Do this even if the windows are small. Do it even if there aren't any windows.

✳ Buy stiff designer bedcovers, 800-thread-count linens, inflexible decorative pillows, and the costliest top-name granite-firm mattresses. All your beds will now be impossible to sleep on, but no matter. They're the best.

✳ Furnish your formal dining room with a table big enough to host an inaugural banquet. Never, Godforbid, use it. It is an ironclad Jewish tradition to squeeze guests around a kitchen table while the dining room set gleams in untouched splendor.

✳ Display collections of dishes, glassware, and table linens you're keeping for a special occasion. Never have an occasion that's special enough.

✳ A popular technique for your bedroom and living room is combining fabric-covered items in patterns and colors that match but don't match—stripes with checks, polka dots with prints, red with pink, pewter with putty. Do not make the mistake of randomly selecting these—Ralph Lauren you're not. They have to exactly don't match.

✳ You would never be so crass as to select artwork by any artificial criterion. But can you help it if the paintings you fall in love with just happen to match your color scheme?

COLORS

There are two categories of Jewish colors.

1. Edible Nouns. A couch of *mushroom* watered silk matches drapes with a thread of *carrot*. A *persimmon* bath rug complements *casaba* towels.

2. Meaningless Nouns. These give you no idea what the color is: *gossamer, loam, mist, wind, breath, sigh.* You will be expected to converse with furniture salespeople as follows: "Do you have that boudoir chair in *mosquito*? The *gunpoint* clashes with my *hula hoop* broadloom."

Some colors are never Jewish, such as powder blue.

22 THiNGS YOU WON'T FiND iN A JEWiSH CLOSET

1. Bowling shoes

2. A one-size-fits-all garment

3. Camouflage-print clothes actually meant to keep you from getting shot

4. A bustier

5. A casino T-shirt

6. Work boots

7. Hats that say things like "I got this for my wife! Good trade, huh?"

8. Wire hangers

9. Samsonite

10. A tie that has dirty words in Chinese letters

11. Shoes not in boxes

12. Fishnet thigh highs

13. Faux anything

14. Overalls

15. Fewer than five bathrobes

16. Clip-on ties

17. Moth repellents that smell like mothballs

18. Goofy or Mickey slippers

19. Wife beaters

20. Goth anything

21. High-top sneakers

22. A homosexual

YOUR JEWISH KITCHEN

YOUR PRIMARY KITCHEN RESPONSIBILITY IS TO KEEP THE room looking as if it's never used. Since a Jewish kitchen is used relentlessly, this is difficult, but with practice you'll learn the proper rhythm.

✳ Have a sponge in your hand at all times. Immediately wipe up any drop of anything that spills anywhere.

✳ It is not enough to simply wash dishes. Scrub them clean before putting them in the dishwasher.

✳ Don't leave a dirty dish for a nanosecond. From the moment you remove it clean from its cabinet, your goal is to use, wash, dry, and return it as swiftly as is humanly possible.

✳ Think of a creative place to hide your trash can. You'll know you have a good spot when someone trying to find it has to open six doors and finally ask where it is.

✳ Constantly mop the floor. People *walk* there, for God's sake.

COOKING

No matter how good you are in the kitchen—even if you're a finalist on *Top Chef* or a culinary school instructor—you'll need to junk everything you thought you knew about cooking. Your new rules:

1. Meat and Poultry. The first two hours of cooking are just to make sure it's dead. Add another three hours—more if someone's stuck in traffic.

2. Vegetables. Don't use fresh ones, they're not sanitary. Canned, you don't know what got processed in there along with the food (Tina on the assembly line is going to stop the belt and remove wormy tomatoes?). Frozen, same.

3. Potatoes and Rice. Make these instead. Cook the hell out of them. Use no seasoning, butter, or anything else that might destroy their tastelessness.

KITCHEN TERMS
YOU NEED TO KNOW

Not sanitary Acceptable for a research laboratory or operating room, but not for a Jewish kitchen ("Don't eat that grape off the counter! It's not sanitary.")

On the stove In imminent danger of being ruined ("Come home right now! Dinner's on the stove!")

On the table About to spoil ("Hurry up—dinner's on the table!")

Cold Worse than spoiled ("Eat! Eat! It's going to get cold!")

4. Fruits. Buy only organic ones. Distrust them anyway. Scrub them, rub them, peel them. While eating them, think about the risk you're taking. As soon as you're done eating, reread the *Seven Danger Signals of Cancer*.

5. Matzo Balls. These should look as imperfect as possible. If you sneak purchased ones into your soup, squeeze and misshape them until they are solidly compacted and leaden. They must show the imprints of exhausted Jewish fingers.

SUPERMARKET FRESHNESS DATES

Whereas non-Jews sniff foods that have been in their refrigerators for eight or nine weeks, Jews hunt for supermarket freshness dates as avidly as we do for suspicious moles. As a newly minted Jew, proceed this way:

✱ At the market, bypass items in the front of the display—these are for the Gentiles.

✱ Reach way around back for the newest ones. Get an employee's help if necessary.

✱ Compare expiration dates.

✱ If none are dated more than two months in the future, ask the manager why there's no fresh stock.

Dented Cans

Non-Jews can eat from these with no problem. Jews get sick just from having a dented can in the house.

✱ At home, conduct a kitchen pogrom at least three times a week, discarding any foods you're at all concerned about, like a carton of milk the dog barked at.

KITCHEN EQUIPMENT

Small Appliances. Have them for every purpose—an electric knife, juicer, bread maker, food processor, blender, coffee grinder, milk foamer, etc. But don't use any of them. Explain with a weary smile that the job is easier/faster/tastier/ more sanitary if done by hand.

Perfect Containers for Leftovers. These are sturdy somethingware bowls and boxes shaped for every conceivable food. Make sure you have pickle-size for pickles, elongated for celery, and so on. They have lock-on lids and vacuum seals, and are guaranteed to maintain freshness for weeks, but

THE MICROWAVE: IS IT REALLY CARCINOGENIC?

Don't stop using it—you need it, for God's sake. Just repeat the customary questions and disclaimers to yourself every time you put something in there (again, this is so God knows that *you* know):

* "They *say* these are safe, but . . ."

* "Didn't they once say *cigarettes* were safe?"

* "Should I stand farther away from it?"

* "Do I already have cancer from *not* standing away from it?"

no Jewish person would believe such bushwa. Empty yours after twelve hours.

A Beautiful, Gleaming, Costly, High-Tech Electric Coffeemaker That Makes Absolutely Putrid Coffee.

Cookbooks. Have several shelves of these. Keep adding the most current ones. Lug them from house to house as you move. Never open them.

Spice Rack. A decorative shelf containing pretty bottles. Mount yours on a wall or on a countertop. Do not, Godforbid, use any of the spices in it. Do you want to be doubled over with gas pains?

Spoon Rest. This is a concave plastic or ceramic flower kept on the counter. The spoon used to stir a cooking pot is rested there between stirrings. If you have difficulty understanding why having yet another sticky, dirty item to wash after a big meal is preferable to simply wiping the counter, this is because you weren't born Jewish.

REALLY TRUE JEWISH MOMENT

My own wonderful grandmother Mollie Goldenberg Chuckrow, may she rest not in peace but in the drama and pandemonium she lived for, asked me one day whether I wanted coleslaw or potato salad with my lunch.

I picked coleslaw.

"Why?" she demanded. "What's the matter with potato salad?"

17 THiNGS YOU WON'T SEE iN A JEWiSH HOME

1. A Lay-Z-Boy

2. A linoleum knife

3. Chef Boyardee

4. A standby ticket

5. Trout flies

6. A Tony Robbins CD

7. Boxing gloves

8. A copy of *He's Just Not That into You* (what nice Jewish girl would ever consider such a possibility?)

9. A Fluffernutter

10. A snow shovel

11. Pop-Tarts

12. A whoopee cushion

13. A rottweiler

14. A Roomba

15. *Accounting for Dummies*

16. A tin of Skoal

17. Spaces where teeth once were

ViSiTiNG SOMEONE'S HOME

PREVIOUSLY, YOU VISITED PEOPLE'S HOMES FOR MANY reasons. As a Jew, you will visit people to **eat.** Though you're experienced with both visiting and eating, this will not be a simple area to master. Be on the alert for the following surprises.

BET-YOU-NEVER-THOUGHT- i-COULD-MAKE-YOU-FEEL-THiS-GUiLTY

YOU: "Sorry we're late. We hit traffic."

YOUR HOSTESS: "My God, I never should have told you to come at four!"

YOU: "It's okay. We just—"

YOUR HOSTESS: "What a total idiot I am! I forgot about the pool traffic! God! I can't do anything right!"

YOU: "Nonsense. Everything's fine."

YOUR HOSTESS: "Watch the chicken. I'm going to take a Xanax."

THE PERiSHABLES RODEO

After you've been in your new Jewish family for a while, you'll automatically respond with horror anytime the word *perishable* is uttered. Its nearest synonym is *botulism.* When a Jewish person notes that a food is perishable, it is assumed to have already perished.

As a guest in a Jewish home, you are obligated to notice and call attention to perishable foods left out of the refrigerator. To do this, you must learn to identify the odor of a dish that might be starting to come close to nearing the condition of possibly approaching the likelihood of beginning to spoil within the next few weeks.

HOW TO TAKE CONTROL iN SOMEONE ELSE'S HOUSE

OF COURSE YOU'RE THE KING OR QUEEN OF YOUR OWN castle. But as a Jewish person, you are now responsible for making sure any house you enter suits your needs—and, if it doesn't, correcting errors or deficiencies that affect your comfort. This is your birthright.

Say Miriam's mother passed away, and you're paying a *shiva*[1] call at Miriam's home. Upon entering, hug Miriam quickly while evaluating the conditions inside. Pay close attention to these crucial factors:

✱ the level of heat or air-conditioning

✱ the lighting

✱ whether windows are open or closed

✱ the presence of any allergens such as pets, smoke, or flowers

✱ the acceptability of any foods or beverages offered

✱ odors or sounds not to your liking

Now is the time to make all necessary changes, before Miriam assumes you're satisfied. It's your responsibility to

✱ adjust the thermostat and light switches

✱ position windows to your preference

---

[1] **Shiva:** Think *wake,* but with more food, no booze, much guilt, and no laughs.

* instruct someone to get rid of any odors, music, or irritating children or pets detrimental to your health

* secure nourishment for yourself, whether this requires removing plastic wrap from dishes on display but not yet served, or hurrying into the kitchen with raised eyebrows and an expressive shrug

HOW TO COMMENT ON SOMEONE'S HOME

About outdoor furniture: "You're going to cover this?"

About dark carpeting: "But it shows the dirt."

About a new appliance (with a knowing sigh): "Save the warranty."

About an exquisitely decorated nursery (with eyes rolled): "Just wait."

About a white anything: "You're going to cover this?"

JEWISH GUEST BEHAVIOR

When visiting your new relatives and friends, you will encounter situations that seem familiar. Your impulse will be to handle them in the familiar way. Do not make this mistake.

Here are some lessons:

Situation 1
(Women Only)

You've brought your special coconut cream pie to the dinner party. As you arrive, your hostess is dashing around the kitchen preparing the meal.

Old Behavior. You discreetly slip the pie into the refrigerator and leave the kitchen.

New Behavior. Loudly announce you've brought the pie as soon as you walk in. Keep talking on your way to the kitchen. Grab the hostess and show her. Tell her how you made it. Don't leave out any of the delicious details. Ask where the heavy cream is. Have her get a beater so you can whip the cream. Show her how you mound the whipped cream on top of the pie, and grate the coconut over it. When you're done, take things out of the refrigerator to make room for the pie. Leave them out.

Situation 2
(Women Only)

You're at a new relative's holiday dinner. Nearly everyone has finished eating. You'd like to help clear.

Old Behavior. You wait till the last person is done, then carry plates to the kitchen. Everyone moves to the living room. Later, before leaving, you offer to help wash. The hostess declines.

New Behavior. About now the hostess will rise and reach for the plates of those who are finished. Stand next to her and help as she scrapes food onto one plate and stacks the others. Keep glancing at those still eating to see if they're done yet. Only when all dishes are scraped, stacked, and organized can you bring them to the kitchen.

The men, and any women who don't care about their reputations, will retire to the family room for TV and conversation about what's on the TV. The real women will bulldoze the kitchen, washing, wiping, and wrapping leftover food to the tune of such favorites as "It's a Crime to Throw This Out," "Let the Glasses Air-Dry—It's More Sanitary," and "Don't You Have a Tupperware Arugula Container?"

Situation 3

You're a dinner guest. You've brought a huge tin of anchovies for a gift (you have a relative in the restaurant-supply business).

Old Behavior. You present the gift, eat, and leave.

New Behavior. Before the dinner, mention often that you're bringing something great. When you arrive, insist that the hostess serve the anchovies immediately. Ask if she has capers. Suggest she roll each anchovy around one. Watch while she does it. She might miss some.

Direct the other guests' attention to the anchovies. Don't let them get distracted by the other hors d'oeuvres. During the meal, remind everyone a few times how good the anchovies were. When you leave, ask the hostess if she *really* enjoyed them. Hint that you might bring something even better next time.

FOOD OAQs

"Is there any mercury in this flounder?"

"Do you want to die of starvation?"

"A hamster, you think that salad could nourish?"

"Can saltines go bad?"

"Who knows how long this ketchup has been sitting out?"

"How can you tell if you have trichinosis?"

"Why didn't you eat the crust?"

"Does this fork look greasy to you?"

"Are the lemons clean?"

"Why does my napkin smell funny?"

Situation 4

You're a first-time guest in someone's home, and you're sniffling. It must be your cat allergy.

Old Behavior. You take an antihistamine and have fun anyway.

New Behavior. Ask accusingly if they have a cat. Proclaim that you're violently allergic. When they offer to put the cat in another room, say it's too late. Ask what medications they have. Reject them all. Describe the details of your allergy. Use up a box or two of tissues. When the topic shifts, sneeze louder.

Situation 5

You're a guest at Melody's dinner party. As she serves the first course, Melody announces: "This is terrible soup."

Old Behavior. N/A. Situation is exclusive to Jewish gatherings.

New Behavior. Say nothing. Melody always does this, and the other guests all know their lines. You'll hear "Why does she always do this?" and "We haven't even tasted it" and "You're right, Mel, we already hate the whole meal." Anything you said would be as disruptive as if you leaped onstage during *Les Miz* and yodeled.

5 THINGS YOU CAN COUNT ON HEARING AROUND A JEWISH TABLE

1. "But that's the best part!" (Said while pointing at a broccoli stem or scaly, footlike hunk of chicken left on your plate.)

2. "Sit down, [hostess]! She never sits down!" (Always said by someone who never gets up.)

3. "I should have made more."

4. "You always make too much."

5. "Don't fill up on bread." (Said by parents to children, spouses to each other, and the hostess to everybody.)

REALLY TRUE
NON-JEWISH MOMENT

Two ladies of the non-Jewish persuasion stop for a late lunch at an outdoor seafood restaurant before going to visit a postsurgical friend at her home.

Among the dishes ordered is giant scallops wrapped in bacon with a Gorgonzola cream sauce. The woman eats one scallop, then pushes the plate aside because it's "too rich."

The meal continues through coffee, dessert, and cordials. The plate remains on the table. The air temperature is 93 degrees.

Finally the scallops are packed in an aluminum take-out container, which is placed in the trunk of their car, which has been parked in the sun.

On the way to the visit, they stop at a drugstore to buy Hershey's Kisses for the patient. As long as they're there, they pick up some other things.

The car is still in the sun, and it's still 93 degrees out.

Arriving at the patient's home, they remove the scallops from the trunk and present the container to the patient, along with the candy, as a gift.

CHAPTER 3

Entertainment

WORRYING

BEFORE YOU WERE JEWISH, YOU PROBABLY SPENT TIME EACH day on your entertainment—jogging, painting, reading. You are fortunate to have this routine established, because it won't be hard to fit in your new entertainment—worrying. Of course, you'll have to forgo the jogging, but which is more important?

Natural-born Jews leave the womb equipped with a worry reservoir that is filled early and replenished constantly. We worry about everything. Worrying is as essential to our well-being as a balanced breakfast. It is our duty, our birthright, and our most profound satisfaction. There are no exceptions to this rule. *All Jews worry all the time.* If there is nothing handy to worry about, we are breath-stoppingly creative at finding something. You will need daily practice to build your worrying skills. Think of this as weight training.

HOW TO WORRY

You may choose from four basic methodologies.

Personal. Select an inconsequential remark someone makes to you. Magnify it out of all proportion. Manufacture nuances the person never dreamed of conveying. Keep agonizing until you manage to convince yourself that because of all this stress you are going to get cancer and die.

Political. Watch the news on TV. Ignore the national headlines and fasten on a story about a fish-processing plant releasing toxins into the air in a remote, barely inhabited Arctic village. Be certain these toxins are finding their way to your neighborhood, and you are going to get cancer and die.

Economic. Buy a stock that drops and leaves you without a nickel to your name (i.e., you can't do a third week on St. Bart's). Work long into the night trying to balance your budget. Get a terrible headache and take aspirin. Be positive the pills are eating away at your digestive tract, and you are going to get cancer and die.

Environmental. Hear a pattering on your roof. Be certain that a planeload of Peruvian Paralyzer Bees, bound for an experimental laboratory, has accidentally been released over your house. So toxic is their venom that you need only be near the insects for your fingers and tongue to go numb, as yours are right now. Be convinced that the numbness is causing a genetic mutation, and you are going to get cancer and die.

WHEN TO WORRY

Lying awake at night is traditional. But morning worry makes a nice change of pace:

✱ You're fresher.

✱ You can be near the refrigerator.

✱ You can phone people and worry *them*.

✱ You can worry that you *will* lie awake all night.

WHAT TO DO iF YOU RUN OUT OF WORRiES

Engaging in everyday conversation with a natural-born Jewish person will provide lots of new material. If that isn't feasible, simply make an enormous big deal out of some existing minor problem, such as:

✱ A slow leak in a tire (You might have a blowout on the highway, and it could be snowing so hard a tractor-trailer couldn't stop, and you'd get hit and die.)

✱ An ingrown toenail (It could get bad enough that you'd have to wear special shoes. But those wouldn't go with your business clothes, and you'd be fired for looking unkempt. Then you'd lose your medical insurance, get blood poisoning, and die.)

✱ An overdrawn account (Creditors would foreclose, your house would be boarded up, you'd break in to retrieve something you forgot, cut yourself on a rusty nail, get lockjaw, and die.)

ALL-PURPOSE "ANYTiME" WORRiES

On rare occasions it may happen that nothing worrisome is going on around you. Should this occur, there is still a veritable garden of oys and veys available to you anywhere you look. From having to eat deviled eggs in a non-Jewish home ("How can I get to see the date on the egg carton?") to too-short pantyhose ("Only a troll, these would fit! Or is it me?") to a computer glitch ("Can you believe I lost my guest list for the Purim coffee?"), prospective qualms abound. In a pinch, you can choose from the following:

An Upcoming Holiday. Let's say New Year's Eve is right around the corner. Torture yourself (and your loved ones) this way:

"Will I have as much fun as last year?"

"If I have *more* fun, will I be disappointed *next* year?"

"Should I take a cab, to avoid the drunks?"

"What if one of the drunks hits the *cab*?"

A Theme Park Visit. You're taking the family to Ten Flags over Duluth. Never mind "gimme" worries like rain and sun. Be original:

"Is $1,200 enough to bring?"

"What if we lose one of the kids?"

"Will the bathrooms be disgusting?"

"How far away will we have to park?"

"What if we get stuck on one of the rides?"

"Are the snack bars in the shade?"

Buying a New Car. Oy, think of it—the schlepping around, the lying salespeople, the numbers they run past you at the speed of light . . . and:

"What if I miss the old car?"

"How long will the new-car smell last?"

"What if I can't park it far from other cars?"

"Will dark leather hold the heat?"

"Will light leather get dirty?"

Your Breath. You're at a nice Italian restaurant.

"Should I tell the waitress to leave out the garlic?"

"Will the shrimp scampi still taste good if they leave it out?"

"What if they put garlic in anyway?"

"What if nobody wants to kiss me ever again?"

TWO-PERSON WORRYiNG (JEWiSH PiNG-PONG)

Player #1: "My sister broke her leg."

Player #2: "*My* sister broke her *engagement*."

Player #1: "An engagement isn't like a *leg*."

Player #2: "Of course not. A leg *heals*."

FUN

YOU THOUGHT THIS WAS A NO-BRAINER, DIDN'T YOU? Who has to be taught to have *fun*? You, new Jew, that's who.

WHAT NON-JEWS DO FOR FUN	WHAT JEWS DO
Visit a relative in Myrtle Beach	Visit a relative in the ICU
Eat a handful of M&M's	Eat a handful of Prilosec
Contra dance	Contradict
Drive monster trucks	Drive other drivers crazy
Eat	Eat and eat and eat
Ride the Cyclone roller coaster	Ride an emotional roller coaster
Take a hike	Take a laxative
Research their family crest	Be crestfallen
Flip people off	Flip out
Join country clubs	Join HMOs
Pick apples	Pick fights
Drink a martini	Drink Metamucil

WHAT NON-JEWS DO FOR FUN	WHAT JEWS DO
Shop for shoes	Shop for a headstone
Have a cat	Have a catastrophe
Eat apple pie	Eat crow
Read the comics	Read the obituaries
Join AA	Join AAA
Criticize another driver	Criticize someone else's doctor
Get your hair done	Get your nose done
Get your boobs done	Get your taxes done

VACATiONiNG

Old (but Still Popular) Tradition

Jews vacation primarily on tropical islands. You are not permitted to enjoy these trips; you will be too busy complaining.

Follow these time-honored rules:

1. Upon landing at your island, be surprised that the local airport isn't air-conditioned.

2. Grumble about the impoverished neighborhoods you pass through on your way to the hotel. Tell the tour guide you didn't come here to be depressed.

3. Run out at dawn to drape towels over the best beach chairs, even if you have no intention of sitting in them. What if you change your mind?

4. Fill your beach bag with every sun protector known to modern science. Smear your body every five minutes. Complain that you're not getting a tan.

5. Be outraged that the natives don't have Lactaid.

6. Worry about crime, bugs, and your drinking water. Know the scientific terms for all the bacteria the water probably contains, and discuss them with other vacationers. Trade cute names for travelers' diarrhea.

REALLY TRUE JEWISH MOMENT

A young woman vacations in Bermuda with a girlfriend. Once home, she tells her mother about a terrible thing that happened there: They were talking to some men at a bar when one of the men suddenly dropped dead.

The mother asks, "What were you *talking* to him about?"

7. Have a minor medical emergency that forces you to get treatment in a ramshackle local hospital. This will be good for years of horror stories.

New (and Increasingly Popular) Tradition

Jews now also travel to places that are dirty, far away, dangerous, hard to get to, and have no edible food, but are very trendy. We do this to one-up each other with tales of our once-in-a-lifetime privileged-access adventures:

"We watched a polar bear give birth on a glacier in Alaska."

"*We* performed a liver transplant in the dark on an endangered spider monkey in Managua."

BEFORE PEOPLE
LEAVE FOR VACATION

Having adopted your new Jewish identity, you must learn to respond appropriately when other people discuss their travel plans.

TRAVELER: "We're taking a trip to Morocco."
NON-JEW: "What an adventure!"
JEW: "Bring Cipro."

TRAVELER: "We're going to Australia."
NON-JEW: "Have a great time!"
JEW: "Australia? Honey, who do we know in Australia?
    Isn't Janice's nephew in Australia?"

TRAVELER: "Cuba, here we come!"
NON-JEW: "Very exciting!"
JEW: "You can text your lawyer from there?"

TRAVELER: "We're going on safari."
NON-JEW: "What fun!"
JEW: "Get shots."

TRAVELER: "We're off to Mexico!"
NON-JEW: "Olé!"
JEW: "Don't eat anything."

TRAVELER: "We're climbing Kilimanjaro."
NON-JEW: "Sounds wonderful."
JEW: "We did that. Without oxygen."

CLASSES OF TRAVEL

As a non-Jew, you probably saw the word *luxury* in a brochure and started packing. However, Jews know that any schlemiel who runs a resort and doesn't work any harder than that to get you there doesn't deserve your money.

When booking a vacation, the key words your Jewish eye must scan for are *palatial, majestic, regal, world-class, ultra exclusive,* or *legendary.* A-List celebrities should go there. Would Matt Damon check into a four-star rat hole?

GETTiNG TO THE AiRPORT

Previously, this was simply a *ride.* To Jews, air travel is an intricate tapestry of whines, worries, and what-ifs:

✳ Twenty-four hours before your flight, begin calling to see if it's on time. Leave for the airport early. Keep calling from the car.

✳ Listen to the traffic reports every 10 minutes—on the 8s on one station, and on the 5s on another.

✳ Shush passengers during each report, even if one is confessing to murder.

✳ Read the road signs aloud to each other. Argue about what they mean.

✳ Once you see the roads are clear and you'll reach the airport early, moan about how bored you're going to be.

SPORTS

TO BE APPROPRIATE FOR A JEWISH PERSON TO ENGAGE IN, a sport must be noisy, competitive, and expensive. Under no circumstance should a sport:

✳ Involve earth.

✳ Need to be played in freezing weather (below 80 degrees).

✳ Draw blood.

✳ Require a shared water bottle.

Favorite Jewish sports include:

✳ Tennis

✳ Racquetball

✳ Golf

✳ Comparing cell phones

✳ Comparing cell phone plans

OTHER LEISURE-TIME ACTIVITIES

PASTIMES YOU ALWAYS THOUGHT WERE RELAXING WILL NOW be the opposite. Where you once sat back and let yourself be entertained, you must now contribute.

TV

You will have to discard your pre-Jewish habit of passive viewing, or your new family will assume you are depressed or sick. The TV screen is meant to provide discussion material.

Hollywood celebrities are a prime topic. You will be expected to join the fun as everyone:

✳ Argues about who that is on the screen.

✳ Reminisces about the movies or TV series she starred in.

✳ Details the plot of each of these movies or series episodes.

✳ Wails about how awful she looks.

✳ Swaps stories of who they know who knows her cousin's doorman.

✳ Bickers over who in the family does, used to, or will someday resemble her.

Active viewing is also required for political talk shows where a bunch of pundits argue and scream at one another. You must join in by arguing with and screaming at the others watching, as well as at the pundits on-screen.

Another popular thing to watch is car commercials. You must learn to be really enthusiastic about these. Get up and join your relatives as they move close to the screen to examine the new models. Contribute to the ensuing critique by describing your friends' experiences with their cars. Relate frightening stories about how unsafe the manufacturing process is. Passionately argue about which model everyone is going to buy next.

Commercials Jews Never Finish Watching

"Dentures stained? Well . . ."

"Nothin' says lovin' like something from the oven . . ."

"I'm not a doctor, but . . ."

"New K-Y Intense. Intensifies female satis . . ."

"Learn how to drive your own big rig . . ."

"Get your GED in just . . ."

"Don't miss the season premiere of *Ghost Hunters*, Friday at . . ."

"Looking for the largest selection of deer rifles in your area? Look no . . ."

"Hamburger Helper helps your hamburger . . ."

"If your erection lasts longer than four hours . . ."

MOVIES

As a non-Jew you had your favorite films. You might have enjoyed screechy car chases, bomb explosions, unnatural natural disasters (St. Louis is suddenly overrun with vampire bats), and so on. These themes are done for you now, as are movies about violence, sex, drunkenness, or, Godforbid, starvation.

YOU MAY WATCH:	BUT NOT:
Evita	Godzilla
Yellow Submarine	I Am Curious (Yellow)
The Proposal	The Hangover
Butterflies Are Free	Last Tango in Paris
Girl, Interrupted	The Girl Most Likely
Blazing Saddles	Fire Down Below
The Purple Rose of Cairo	Death on the Nile
What's Up, Doc?	Dr. Strangelove
Who Framed Roger Rabbit?	Fatal Attraction
Schindler's List	Bucket List

CELEBRiTiES JEWS AREN'T CRAZY ABOUT

Wayne Newton

Sylvester Stallone

Missy "Misdemeanor" Elliott

Hulk Hogan

Dog, the Bounty Hunter

Trace Adkins

the Kardashians

Kid Rock

Lady GaGa

Eminem

Vin Diesel

Rascal Flatts

(Should I bother mentioning Mel Gibson? Nah.)

READiNG BOOKS

Your new Jewish family expects you to be as well-read as they are, so keep up with the new books the same way they do.

Preorder the hottest new release on Amazon. Complain about how long it takes to get it. Complain about the charge for express shipping. Hate the book.

WEEKEND AMUSEMENT

YOUR NEW FAMILY WILL ALWAYS SPEND SATURDAY NIGHT IN the same delightful manner. Here's how to be an effective participant.

1. On Friday, buy a paper. Read the restaurant reviews. Phone the highest-rated one and make a reservation for 8:00 Saturday night.

2. Arrive at 8:10. Indignantly ask why your table isn't ready. Be horrified at the size of the crowd waiting at the bar.

3. At 8:15, start to badger the headwaiter.

4. At 8:30, announce that the place is poorly run.

5. At 8:45, threaten to write a letter to the paper.

6. When you're finally seated, criticize the table, the food, and the service.

7. Repeat all steps the following week (preferably at the same restaurant).

An alternate Saturday night activity is to make several restaurant reservations and select at your leisure. Don't bother canceling the ones you won't keep. You don't want to waste your evening making phone calls.

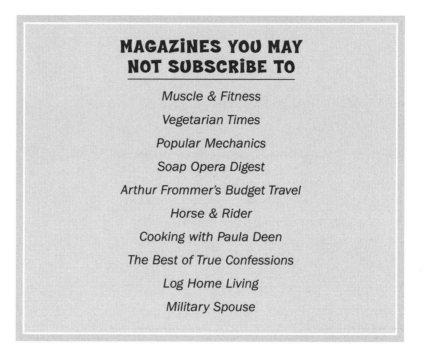

MAGAZiNES YOU MAY NOT SUBSCRiBE TO

Muscle & Fitness

Vegetarian Times

Popular Mechanics

Soap Opera Digest

Arthur Frommer's Budget Travel

Horse & Rider

Cooking with Paula Deen

The Best of True Confessions

Log Home Living

Military Spouse

GOiNG TO ENJOYABLE EVENTS

THE MOST IMPORTANT PART OF ATTENDING AN EVENT IS **leaving.** You will never again see the end of a concert, the last act of a play, or the ninth inning of a ballgame. You *must* beat the crowd out of the venue, the parking lot, and the roads. This is the one and only way the success of the experience is measured.

SONGS YOU'LL NEVER HEAR A JEWISH PERSON SING

"Wild Thing"

"When the Bullet Hits the Bone"

"I Love the Nightlife"

"I Can't Stay Mad at You"

"One Bourbon, One Scotch, One Beer"

"Third-Rate Romance, Low-Rent Rendezvous"

"I Fought the Law and the Law Won"

"Sex Machine"

"Some Guys Have All the Luck"

(**You *will* hear us sing any of the following, however:** "It's My Party and I'll Cry If I Want To," "I've Gotta Be Me," and everyone's favorite, "I'll Never Smile Again.")

At exactly the right moment, your group will jump from their seats and hurry up the aisle. One of you will yell, "Run! Run!" as if you are being chased by fire ants.

If someone is lucky enough to discover a side door, this will be as if Tiffany's opened its doors just for you and told you to take whatever you wanted.

SiTTiNG

One of the few full-body physical activities embraced by Jews is **sitting.** This is a lot more complicated than it seems, because **where to sit** is a major negotiation, the object of which is to win your preferred seat by using your personal ailment to trump other participants. For example:

Larry can't sit in the sun. Amy can't sit in the back of the car. Sharon has to sit at the end of a row. Left-handed Steve can't sit next to a right-handed person.

Larry only wins if he's had skin cancer, or thought he had it. Amy has to threaten to throw up, not just get dizzy. Sharon wins if she's been officially diagnosed (by another Jewish person) as claustrophobic. Steve loses, since inconvenience, while it is a tragedy, is bested by danger.

Nobody wants to sit at a round table, because it's too hard to hear. Nobody wants to sit at a rectangular table, because it's too hard to see. Nobody wants to sit near the band. Everybody wants to sit close to the bathroom. But not too close.

Once seated, if you're not comfortable, which no Jew ever is, use grunts and sighs and body language to illustrate your distress. Some traditional techniques:

PROBLEM	INDICATOR
The sun is in your eyes.	Squint. Cover your eyes, alternating hands as each gets tired. Try to block the torment by leaning your upper body in all directions. Don't succeed.
The air conditioner is blowing on you.	Shiver. Say, "Brrrrrr." Pull whatever you're wearing tighter around you. Cross your arms and legs. Rub your shoulders. Flaunt your goose bumps.
The seat hurts your back.	Ostentatiously massage the painful area while making agonized sounds and twisting your face into a tortured mask.
You're too near the music.	Grimace, cover your ears, and lean your head down as far into your lap as you can. Shout every word you say.
You just can't get comfy.	Twist your body from side to side. Lift each butt cheek in turn. Cross, uncross, and recross your legs.

The final act of this play is **Jewish Musical Chairs.** This is what you'll hear:

"Ashley, is that sun too bright? Let's switch seats."

"But then it'll be in *your* eyes."

"Aunt Bea, are you catching a chill?"

"Well, I *did* just get over pneumonia."

"Everybody, look, Ethel has a bad back."

"Sit here, Ethel. You like music, don't you?"

"Fred, you look miserable in that chair."

"I'll survive."

"No, you won't. Ashley, change seats with Fred."

DINING AT
OUTDOOR RESTAURANTS

Of course you and your new family love alfresco meals. You'll want to maximize the experience by selecting a place to eat where the environment is completely natural. That's what you came for—to sit on tree stumps, use disposable tableware, and generally enjoy the delights of the outdoors.

But it's your duty to make employees aware of anything that limits your dining pleasure. If the restaurant features outside seating, they must be prepared to meet any obstacles to the experience.

Before the appetizers even arrive, feel free to advise the staff,

"The bugs are terrible!"

"It's so windy, my napkin flew away!"

"Is it always so hot?"

"My seat is damp."

"There are leaves on the table."

"It's so noisy out here."

"I think I just saw a snake."

HAVING PEOPLE OVER

YOU MUST SHED ANY POLLYANNA ILLUSIONS REMAINING FROM your pre-Jewish years about the purpose of entertaining. A Jewish person would never invite people over for ridiculous reasons like *having fun* or *treating friends*. Appropriate reasons include:

✳ **Guilt** (The same person has hosted the last three *seders*,[1] and it wasn't you.)

✳ **Pain** (Someone copied your Meyer lemon crème brûlée, and hers came out better.)

✳ **Obligation** (Everybody in your body-sculpting class has done a brunch, and you're getting looks.)

✳ **Duty** (Your child is the only one in his grade who hasn't had a theme birthday party exciting enough for the newspaper to cover.)

✳ **Resentment** (Your cousin had the gall to imply that only she can do *Bucatini alla Amatriciana* right, when you're the one who's brilliant at it.)

✳ **Pressure** (Your parents-in-law call daily to see if you've set the date for their surprise anniversary party.)

---

[1] **Seder:** A dinner we have at Passover, one of the few joyous Jewish traditions. Our non-mournful holidays all have the same theme: They tried to kill us, we won, let's eat.

WHEN YOU HAVE A PARTY

Invitations. You must shop exhaustively for yours. Find the cutest, most original ones. Have them professionally printed in a manner that highlights any especially splendid details, such as "Cocktails on the colonnade, with music by L'Orchestre d'Expense Extrême." Any guest who doesn't compliment your invitation should never be invited again.

Include something adorable in the envelope, like little stars or sequins that fall out when it's opened. This will upset recipients who aren't standing directly over a wastebasket at the time, but no matter—it's a precious touch.

Sylvia The home of a couple in which that is the woman's name ("Are we going to Mildred Saturday?" "No, we're going to Sylvia.")

The invitation will give an RSVP date weeks or months hence. However, guests are expected to respond right away, both to say they're coming and to *kvel*[2] over your cuteness. If they can't come, press them as to why.

Only non-Jews think the RSVP date means they can wait to respond. Immediately start badgering people who haven't called upon receipt.

Say no when they ask if they can bring anything. Be hurt if they don't.

Pre-Invitations. At certain festive times of year, people start picking off others' Saturdays. You mustn't let this happen to you. Do you want only unpopular guests at your party?

Here is how to make your social end run:

Four or five months before the wedding or shower or whatever, have a darling fridge magnet made. This should have something on it like two bunnies kissing and should say, "Brianna and Hollis, June 21—Save the Date!" Send one to each guest.

Now you have put dibs on people. Once they get one of these, they're pretty much roped in. Of course, the same goes for you. So if Felice's wedding in Maui is on the same January Saturday as Kyle's bar mitzvah in Buffalo, you better hope Felice's parents send their magnet first.

---

[2] **Kvel:** Admire (usually way more than the object deserves).

THE POLITICS OF ENTERTAINING

Far from being fun, entertaining is a power play. As host, you are President-for-a-Day. This leaves guests in the position of having to please you, flatter you, compete for your attention, and pretend to be closer to you than anyone else there.

So you can't blame them for reacting by engaging in some power games of their own, with you and with one another.

The Counterfeit-Concern Ploy

You're all sitting around the family room. Estelle, a guest, asks several people, one by one, whether they're cold. They all say no. "The air conditioner isn't blowing on you?" she asks. They shake their heads. Estelle nods, relieved that everybody is comfortable, but still looks troubled. She waits patiently.

Finally someone says, "Are *you* cold, Estelle? Maybe we should turn the air conditioner off."

"That's a good idea," Estelle says.

The Real-Thing Regatta

Variation A: Everybody is happily snarfing down your wonderful lunch when someone says, "Look—poor Flo spilled soup on her silk blouse."

Flo must now either admit she's wearing faux or undergo the seltzer-and-angst ritual of removing a spot from silk. If she tries to hedge, someone else will do the follow-up: "Do you think it'll come out, Flo?"

Variation B: You're asked, "Do you have a little Hellmann's for this sandwich?"

The speaker wants to contrast her fine taste with your minginess when you bring out your Stop & Shop mayo. Don't get too excited if you happen to have Hellmann's. She'll get you on something else.

The Close Call

A guest slips on a drop of water on the kitchen floor. She catches herself, but her gasp can be heard in Laos. After the Oh-my-God chorus, the Are-you-all-right refrain, and the No-wonder-she-slipped-this-floor's-sopping-wet reprise, the incident is forgotten.

But only for ten minutes.

Each new arrival will be warned about the dangerous floor. He or she will question the victim. Similar experiences will be related, escalating in severity.

When it's time to leave, each guest will remind you to be sure to do something about that death-trap floor.

OUTDOOR ENTERTAINING

The Cookout, or *bobbycue,* is a casual form of carefree outdoor entertaining, the object of which is to go to far more trouble than if you were serving a meal indoors. These parties take place in boiling-hot weather and usually include young children, who run inside with the mustard, ketchup, and melting desserts that you had hoped to protect your furniture from (the main reason you planned your outdoor dinner in the first place).

Here's how to make a bobbycue:

1. Buy an enormous, heavy, ostentatious, stainless steel gas grill. This device performs the amazing feat of leaving you with plenty of black gunk to clean up, while producing food with no barbecue flavor whatsoever—the ideal Jewish outdoor cooking appliance.

2. Make inconvenient trips to distant stores for foods such as custom-ground veal sausage. It would be a crime to serve such delicacies with French's, so be sure to provide four or five varieties of mustard.

3. Serve your paper plates in wicker holders. Plastic cutlery and cups must be washed and put away for next time.

4. Do not spoil anyone's fun by trying to change the subject when your guests debate whether barbecued foods cause cancer.

5. Once the guests have left, keep running outdoors to make sure the grill has cooled, the gas is sealed, and you haven't overlooked any spills that could, Godforbid, attract bugs.

GiFTS

JEWS GIVE GIFTS FOR EVERY OCCASION. OCCASIONS INCLUDE not only birthdays and weddings, but also college acceptances, weight loss, and the like. Sometimes we ask others' opinions on whether or not to bring a gift, but we always do, no matter what the advice was.

Some pointers on giving and receiving:

✳ Every gift you get will have strings attached. You will never understand what those are.

✳ Your new relatives would never be so insensitive as to give you a gift certificate. That would deprive you of the joy of criticizing the gift, agonizing over how to say you're exchanging it, schlepping it to the store, and arguing about the store's return policy.

✳ Select gifts for your new family with great care. They won't like anything, but that's no excuse not to drive yourself insane hunting down a better present than anyone else will give.

GiFT GUiDELiNES

TYPE OF GIFT	SUITABLE	UNSUITABLE
Candy	Large, rich artisanal chocolates lumpy with nuts, or hand-dipped berries	Gumdrop fruit slices
Flowers	Special roses that bloom once every thirty centuries	Arrangement stuck in Styrofoam in a cute pottery animal
Wine	Any good California or French, or an Australian that was just written up	Smirnoff Ice, Bartles & Jaymes Wine Coolers
Food	A kangaroo's-milk cheese, exotic fruit, jams with the labels all in Flemish	Fruitcake, petits fours in a decorated tin
Wedding gift	Any useless sterling or crystal item	The Bullet, a punch bowl, a George Foreman Grill
Baby gift	A pink silk dress or blue suit that has to be dry-cleaned	A battery-operated animal that clacks around the floor and bangs into walls

WHEN A CRISIS HITS

YOU MAY BE WONDERING WHY THIS TOPIC IS COVERED IN the chapter on entertainment, but you're a Jew now, so the world as you once knew it has changed. When you were still a Not, a crisis was something that involved destruction, violence, civil unrest, or a pandemic. This is no longer the case. Thus, you must completely recast your definition of the word.

It is important to recognize the signs of a crisis. Failure to understand and appropriately react to one means your family will consider you heartless. Your partner and his or her extended family has every right to expect you to drop whatever you're doing and ride out the emergency with them. Keep in mind that the same will be done for you the next time you fall apart.

Typical crises include:

✳ Waiting for a repairman ("The cable guy hasn't come yet? Oh, God. I'll be right home.")

✳ The landscaper goofed ("My hostas are all moved around!")

✳ An indispensable appliance just broke ("The Sonicare isn't working. How will I brush my teeth?")

✳ Something important is missing ("I can't find my third pair of golf shoes!")

✳ Plans are altered ("The travel agent wants us to change planes in Pittsburgh instead of Cleveland!")

✳ Not getting the right rental car ("A Neon? I'll have such claustropho—I mean, there's no way . . .")

✳ Having your building variance denied ("Can you believe they want us to make the driveway two inches shorter?")

The appropriate response to these and other crises is based on a sliding scale:

BIGGER CRISIS = GREATER SUFFERING = MORE FUN

ENTERTAINMENT OAQS

"Do they have mosquitoes out there?"

"Why is there a lipstick stain on my glass?"

"Do they have to play the music so loud?"

"What's with this wind?"

"Can Diet Coke cause blurred vision?"

"Why do they have to put sauces on everything?"

"I wonder if the mussels are fresh."

"Who's waiting on us?"

"Why is it so dark in here?"

"The food is terrible. And why such small portions?"

CHAPTER 4

Your New Jewish Body

WHAT GOES ON INSIDE THE JEWISH BODY IS WHAT GIVES us the ability to see, run, breathe, complain, berate, call our sons for a second opinion, make our coleslaw with Splenda, wait in loud agony for blood test results, get to the play forty-five minutes before curtain, and do the thousands of things we do every day. Our body gives us life. It also gives us gas, backaches, hunger, stress, carpal tunnel, pinched nerves, angina, gout, bursitis, and sciatica. But for the Jewish body, that *is* life.

FEEDiNG YOUR NEW JEWiSH STOMACH

YOU CAN'T HAVE FAILED TO NOTICE THAT EVERYONE IN YOUR new family is, to say the ridiculous least, body-conscious. Males and females from infancy to passing away are obsessed with the workings of their bodies—and with everything that journeys through them.

TOXiC SUBSTANCES

The modern Jewish digestive system thrives on simple, natural foods. Staples such as tortellini, pesto, rack of lamb, porcinis, mesquite-and-passionfruit-smoked trout, yuzu vinaigrette, and duck confit make up the average diet.

There are, however, three life-threatening substances that the Jewish stomach must never ingest.

Non-Diet Soda. You needn't worry when in someone's home. Any regular soda is kept in a separate refrigerator and drunk only by the landscaper. But in a public place, you can't be too careful. A Jewish person wouldn't dream of trusting a restaurant soda to be diet. Upon requesting and being served such a drink, you must follow this procedure:

1. Ask the waiter if he's sure it's diet.

2. Taste it. Taste it again. Frown.

3. Have the person next to you taste it.

4. If there's regular soda at the table, taste that. Let your neighbor compare, too. If there's no non-diet, order some. Remember to make sure you're not billed for it.

Non-Decaf Coffee. Follow the steps above anytime you are served alleged decaffeinated coffee outside of the home. Every Jewish family has at least one "expert," and he or she will be glad to sample your cup and render a verdict. Don't trust that opinion either, of course (the expert can't afford the loss of face caused by betraying a doubt). During the whole procedure, keep warning everyone that you're going to be up all night. By the time you've sampled enough real coffee to satisfy yourself that you were, in fact, served decaf, you certainly will be.

Cream. Jews don't put such a thing in their coffee. You have every right to be irritated if a server doesn't know this simple fact. Have her take the cream pitcher away and bring milk. Sniff it. Check for specks. Examine the dispenser with distaste. Decide to drink the coffee black.

WHAT GOES INTO YOUR NEW JEWISH MOUTH

YOU USED TO ENJOY:	BUT NOW YOU MUST HAVE:
Spiral-cut ham	Prosciutto di Parma
Marshmallow fluff	Crème fraîche
Miracle Whip	Aioli
Bud	Beaujolais
Squid	Squab
Chicken-fried steak	Steak tartare
Pretzels	Unsalted dry-roasted macadamias
A sandwich	A wrap
Lipton	Lapsang Souchong

JEWISH COMFORTS

Hot drink Something Jews press on you in circumstances where non-Jews would provide a *real* drink (e.g., after a car accident or pit bull attack).

Coffee A meal, served at any time of the day or evening, that consists of at least two kinds of pastry, cookies, and sliced fruit. The fruit cancels out the calories in the pastry.

CHINESE FOOD

For no reason that has ever been clear to anyone, Jewish people adore Chinese food. As foreign as caffeine and cream are to our bodies, soy sauce is our cure. Never mind chicken soup; when Jews need comfort, solace, or medicinal nourishment, we dive for moo shu pork.

Chinese treats may be enjoyed anytime, but there are two nights on which Jews flock to Chinese restaurants: Thursday (because it's the housekeeper's night off) and Sunday (because we just do).

Two No-Win Negotiations

1. (Loser: The Waiter) You are in a Szechuan restaurant. Hot-and-spicy dishes are starred on the menu. Different-color stars indicate grades of spiciness. Someone in your group asks the waiter how hot a certain dish really is: very, very hot or just hot? Someone else asks whether medium-hot means more medium or more hot.

The waiter does his best to answer these questions. He asks everyone how much spiciness is desired and makes careful notes. Each diner insists on plenty of spice. No one wants food that's too mild. Tales are swapped about the blandness of Szechuan dishes at other restaurants.

When the food comes, everyone sends it back because it's much too hot.

2. (Loser: You) You're in someone's kitchen deciding on a takeout order. Foods are suggested. Everyone seems to deliberate before picking.

You're asked what you'd like. You say everything they've chosen sounds great. They press. There must be *something* you want.

Eager to be polite, you demur. You're told you might as well pick, since another dish is needed and everyone else has named something.

Clearly, it would be rude not to contribute. Beef with snow peas, you say.

There's a thunderclap of silence. Everyone looks over or around you. Chairs squeak.

Finally someone points out that there's a beef dish already, two if you count the Land and Sea.

You don't know what to do. Sweating, you suggest peanut chicken.

No. Anita has diverticulitis. No nuts.

Someone else says, Let's get this over with, how about another large spare ribs? They all turn to you for agreement.

You'd agree at this point to chopped ashtrays in garlic sauce. You sigh in relief and nod.

Eventually you will realize that, as with negotiations at so many Jewish get-togethers, this game is ancient. These people were ordering Chinese food together when you still thought sesame was something on a Big Mac bun. They always order the same dishes. And they always end up getting another large spare ribs.

SHARiNG

In your new family, this term applies not only to Chinese entrées but also to the protocol you must observe when your meal doesn't agree with you.

Situation

You've eaten out with a relative. Later, you have a gastrointestinal upset.

Old Behavior. You take Pepto-Bismol and go back to sleep.

New Behavior. Immediately call the person you ate with, no matter what time it is, and describe your symptoms in detail. The two of you will review and compare everything you ate, and isolate the likely cause. It's helpful if you recall that one of these foods didn't taste right, and that you knew as soon as you swallowed it that you shouldn't have.

REALLY TRUE JEWiSH MOMENT

When the first *Jewish as a Second Language* was published, I was invited to give a talk following an Israel Bond Organization luncheon. Tense about addressing 500 people, I just picked at the chicken. The organizer looked at my plate in horror. He said, "*Eat! Eat!* You're going to be too *shvach*[1] to speak!"

---

[1] **Shvach:** Weak. Weaker than a non-Jew could ever be.

THE iMODiUM iNViTATiONAL

As a Gentile, you've probably never dreamed of discussing diarrhea with anyone but a gastroenterologist, and then only if your life was at stake. In your new Jewish family, you must learn to converse about bowel habits (yours, someone else's, and those of anyone they know) as often as you do the weather. If you're terribly shy, just say, "*You* know," and point to your behind.

Be prepared to compete. If Morty had six bowel movements, you had ten. If Tanya needed eight doses of Imodium, you needed twelve, and that was along with several Lomotils. This is an especially popular topic following foreign travel, when the Jews in your new family rush to describe their intestinal escapades even before e-mailing everyone the slide show of their trip. An always-fascinating addition to the travel stories is the hilarious dearth of toilets:

"I had to go in a hole in a dirt floor."

"*I* had to ride a donkey three miles to the mouth of an active volcano."

CARING FOR THE REST OF YOUR NEW JEWISH BODY

THERE'S NOTHING WE JEWS RELISH MORE THAN MEDICAL problems—describing them, second-guessing doctors about them, imagining them, fearing them, having them. You will need to develop this all-consuming interest yourself. You will also find that the ailments you do have will be different from those of your pre-Jewish years. Never again will you have a simple *cold*. It will be a *chest cold* or *head cold*. In a Jewish family, you can also have a cold in your *back* or *eye*. Don't question these conclusions. **All Jews are born diagnosticians.**

To prepare for your future colds, you'll have to learn some new behavior.

✱ When someone gets a cold, the whole family has to figure out where it came from. If you're fingered as the carrier because you sneezed once, you must accept the guilt. This is a very damning position for a Jewish person to be in. Don't be surprised to find yourself really nauseous over it.

✱ When someone sneezes, pull up your shirt collar to create a solid germ barrier, and lean in the opposite direction.

✱ Always warn people, "Don't kiss me— I have a cold." This is a cardinal rule, even though you and most of the population and the entire AMA believe that a cold is contagious mainly during incubation. You are all wrong.

✳ A family with a new baby knows you'll cancel plans with them ifGodforbid you come down with a cold. This expectation remains in effect until the child votes.

As your body begins its Jewish functioning, you will swap old problems for new ones.

YOU CAN NO LONGER GET:	BUT YOU CAN GET:
A chain saw injury	A pinched nerve
A shaving cut	Diabetes
Warts	A hiatal hernia
A black eye	A paper cut
Herpes	Depression
An electric shock	Angina
A cut from a can lid	Gas
A toothache	The *symptoms* of any ailment whatsoever

HOW TO CHOOSE A DOCTOR

Your doctor takes care of your body, but also provides crucial information and impressive new medical terms that are essential to pontificating about your own health. After all, *king of the universe* is what the word *doctor* means in Hebrew.

Any doctor whose name doesn't draw an awestruck gasp when you mention it is not famous enough to treat you. This may be the reason Jews tend not to have sudden illnesses; so much research is necessary to find an acceptably unavailable physician.

To be qualified to treat you, a doctor must:

✱ Have a narrow specialty, such as thumb surgery or aortic valve replacement.

✱ Be booked solid for the foreseeable future. (If he has openings when you call, hang up immediately.)

✱ Agree to squeeze you in only because some *macher* [2] phoned him for you.

✱ Keep you waiting at least three hours.

✱ Ridicule any other doctor who told you anything.

✱ Seem surprised that you have questions, and rush you out of his office without answering them.

✱ Send you an outrageous bill.

---

[2] **Macher:** A Jewish person so transcendently important that he or she can actually get a doctor on the phone.

9 THINGS DOCTORS SAY ONLY TO JEWS

Everyone in your new family will gaze up at God and swear the doctor told them in these exact words:

1. "You have the worst sinus infection I've ever treated."

2. "Thank God you got Sam to the hospital in time. Twenty seconds more and his colon would have exploded."

3. "Rest, Barbara. Don't lift a finger, or you'll need massive surgery."

4. "Phyllis, your fibroid is the size of a cantaloupe."

5. "Do you want to live, Norman? Then never go near another shrimp."

6. "Howard's heart stopped twenty-three times during his prostate surgery."

7. "Would you rather die in the hospital or at home? Because if you don't eat your bran, you can take your choice."

8. "On my children's lives, I've never seen a swollen toe this big."

9. "Arlene, you were ten seconds from death."

YOUR JEWISH IMMUNE SYSTEM

All throughout your body, you have security systems to defend it against intruders. But Jewish intruders are different. Some toxic substances affect us only; Gentiles are immune to them. The main one of these offenders is **the weather.**

As all Jews know, the weather conspires to make us sick. It's vital to monitor this enemy. When someone wants to make plans with you, your first response should always be, "We'll see how the weather is." Then stay alert for deadly threats to your health, such as humidity, heat, cold, and rain.

It's also your responsibility to keep yourself and others fully informed of current conditions at all times. Think of this as building a moat around the enemy. Tell family members on their way out, "Be careful. It's freezing/boiling/soaking wet." When someone comes in, ask, "How is it out? Do I need a sweater?" Then add or subtract a layer to or from whatever they suggest, just to be on the safe side. IfGodforbid someone should mislead you, there's no reason to ever speak to them again.

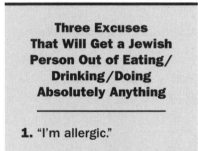

Three Excuses That Will Get a Jewish Person Out of Eating/ Drinking/Doing Absolutely Anything

1. "I'm allergic."

2. "It makes me nauseous."

3. "I'm having blood work."

Finally, exchange data after each outing about how miserable you were in the cold/heat/rain/fog/wind. ("My fingers were literally icicles." "I couldn't keep the car on the road.") Don't spare the adjectives. You don't want to bore people.

THE MEDICINE CHEST

The most important part of the most important room in a Jewish home, the medicine chest is always fully stocked with impressive prescriptions. But don't count on finding the products you were accustomed to in your pre-Jewish days.

YOU WILL FIND:	BUT NOT:
Ambien	Nytol
A Fleet Enema	Efferdent
Extra-strength everything	Toothbrushes with rubber gum stimulators
Jolen Creme Bleach	Nair
Super Extra-Strength Even-for-Mexico Antibacterial Protection Hand Gel	Bag Balm
Maalox Max	Brioschi
Rectal Desitin	IcyHot
Advil	HeadOn
Every laxative there is	Dexatrim

YOUR NEW OUTLOOK
ON HOSPITALS AND ILLNESS

It's a toss-up whether Jews spend more of their time in restaurants or in hospitals. We're enthusiastic about both, but hospitals have the advantage of providing lots to worry about.

In any case, as a member of a Jewish family, you'll have to spend time in them, too. (Not, Godforbid, as a patient. Of 950 Jews in the average medical center at any moment, 918 are visitors. None beneath the rank of Attending Physician are staff.)

Here's what will be expected of you:

✱ Know the visiting hours, medical/surgical/maternity floor designations, and the location of the bakery nearest to all hospitals in your area. (*Area* is defined as your state, and all contiguous states.)

✱ Learn the tricks for getting around the two-visitors-only rule. After you've been in the family awhile, you'll be expected to contribute some new ones.

✱ Be prepared to leave whatever you're doing to accompany your spouse to the hospital when a relative is admitted. If you're trying a case before the Supreme Court and the patient is a ninety-year-old who had a little chest pain after a huge French meal, this still applies.

YOUR HOSPITAL VOCABULARY

Major surgery Any surgery undergone by a Jewish person.

Thenurse A generic term for whatever resource is needed. ("Ask thenurse why there's no dessert on his tray." Or, "He needs a bigger TV. Tell thenurse.")

Agony Discomfort. ("They changed Sheila's bandage. She was in agony.")

Discomfort Agony. ("Thenurse told Marvin to expect discomfort with his disc surgery.")

✱ Never contradict your spouse when he/she tells someone the patient was "rushed to the hospital." This is perfectly accurate even if he walked over in his golf pants.

✱ Never visit without pastry—especially if the patient is on a restricted diet, since there won't be any decent snacks for guests on his meal trays.

✱ Make sure the patient isn't placed with a roommate whose condition could depress him or his guests.

✱ Remember, it's rude to ignore the roommate and his visitors. Find out their first names immediately. Enough pastry should be on hand at all times for both visiting groups. If you arrive and find the roommate without company, it's your duty to cheer him. Draw him out by asking about his condition. Don't be reluctant to mention that you've known people who died of it.

✱ Educate your relative and his roommate on the hideous side effects of their medications. Share any rumors you hear about the hospital's negligence.

✱ If the patient is in Intensive Care, don't worry about those ridiculous ICU visiting regulations. Of course "immediate family" includes his poker group.

MEDICAL PRESTIGE

You must strive to adopt a whole new view of illness and its treatment. You used to feel sympathy and concern for a sick person; now you will need to be impressed. The more complicated the sickness, the more admiring you must be. With years of experience, you should even be able to manage genuine envy.

A patient gains extra prestige when:

✱ The ailment takes its most extreme form. (Perhaps even more extreme than was previously possible. Only Jews can have triple pneumonia or a septuple bypass.)

✱ The problem can't be diagnosed. "The Doctors don't know what's wrong with her" is as awe-inspiring a statement as can be made at the gym. (*The Doctors*, incidentally, are a single entity, a body of learned men who move about and adjudicate as a unit, like bundled cigars.)

✱ He's waiting for the results of what is always a "battery of tests." You can grab some prestige yourself by becoming a waiter or sub-waiter (the person who's waiting to hear from the person who's waiting to hear from the patient, who's waiting to hear from The Doctors).

✱His doctor has status. It's not enough just to be a specialist: As you know, Jews don't go to doctors who aren't specialists. The status doctor must be the "top man in the field." Often he's also one of the "top five in the country." As of now, there are 348 top five urologists in the country.

✱ Certain foods are prohibited. The restriction must be unique enough so the patient can, for example, announce in a restaurant, "Take away that lasagna. The oregano could kill me." For maximum effect, the statement should be made by someone else: "Keep those scallops away from Rose. She could convulse." You must also stay alert for foods that have made you ill before, and impart this information to others ("Like a lobster, my rash was"), as well as remember their allergies. Thus, when Mildred reaches for a raisin scone, you can gently remind her, "You threw up all over my broadloom the last time you ate one of those."

WHEN SOMEONE IS SICK IN THE HOSPITAL

DON'T SAY:	SAY:
"I'm so sorry."	"I'm not surprised."
"I hope you feel better."	"What are they giving you?"
"That should help."	"That's the worst thing they could do."
"Can I do anything for you?"	"Oh, my God. I was with you last week."

WHEN YOU GET SiCK

Jews don't get sick often. This is not due to any genetic factor. It's because we baby ourselves like orphaned seals. There can never be too many sweaters or too much sleep.

But should illness or injury strike you, it's your duty to **stay sick** as long as you can. Keep using those crutches. Prop them up where everyone can see them. Flash that sling. Enlarge that bandage. Who knows when you'll be dealt this card again?

Your illness should progress through stages that determine how you respond to new relatives when they ask how you're feeling. These stages go from most to least extreme:

* Deathly ill
* Acutely ill
* Miserable

* Still miserable
* Tolerable
* Still not right

There is no such answer as *fine*.

HOW TO TAKE AN EKG

1. As soon as the technician hooks up the leads, start asking if your heart is okay.

2. Peer at the printout as it comes from the machine. Freak out over the peaks and valleys. You don't know what these mean, but it can't be good.

3. Ask more questions. Assume anything less than a big smile and a thumbs-up means you're dying.

4. Once you know you'll live, worry that the gucky gel on your chest is going to give you contact dermatitis.

14 THINGS THAT KILL ONLY JEWS

1. Humidity

2. Missing a meal

3. Losing a client ("Cinnabon dropped out. This will kill Ralph.")

4. Flight delays ("We only had fourteen hours to get to the bris. Fran nearly had a heart attack.")

5. Tap water

6. Fast-food fries ("They cook them in lard. *LARD!*")

7. Little Marissa working as a checker at Stop & Shop ("That's it. I'm in my grave.")

8. Going outside with wet hair

9. The drugstore being out of Gas-X

10. Traffic ("Beating the traffic" is as essential as avoiding *E. coli.*)

11. Fatigue ("I'm so tired, I'm dropping dead.")

12. College rejections

13. A scrap of stuffing left inside the turkey

14. Approaching the Mexican border

> **Death**
> ___
>
> Jews do not *die*. We *pass away* or are *gone* or *lost*. The word *anything* is used to signify the possibility of death ("IfGodforbid anything should happen to Hy . . .").

FAMILY TRAITS

O N OCCASION—LET'S SAY, ABOUT EVERY SIX YEARS—YOUR normal . . . I mean, *non-Jewish* relatives may mention a special characteristic of yours, politely noting that it was shared by an ancestor. "Your white-blond hair is lovely," they say. "Grandmother Dolores had it as well."

Jews take this custom to a whole 'nother level. Nothing that you are or have is ever yours alone. Pretty eyes? Thank your great aunt. Good at math? That's Grandpa Baruch for you.

All Jewish traits are family traits. Our obsession with family is second only to our obsession with self. You will never again have a family conversation without numerous references to cousin Hannah's lisp or Uncle Leo's inverted nipples. Whatever we have, we got it from someone.

This is one more of the many lose–lose situations you must be prepared to encounter. Here's why:

Good traits: We get no credit for these. "Aunt Malcha was a brilliant storyteller," a prizewinning journalist is told. "That's why you have a little writing talent." Or, "No wonder your rugelach[3] taste okay. Grandma Rivka baked better than Martha Stewart."

---

[3] **Rugelach:** Pointy, twisty little pastries loaded with sugar, butter, nuts, jam, and everything else we're always telling one another not to eat.

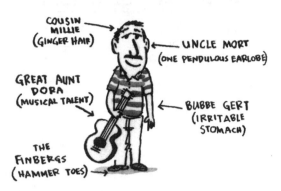

COUSIN MILLIE (GINGER HAIR)

UNCLE MORT (ONE PENDULOUS EARLOBE)

GREAT AUNT DORA (MUSICAL TALENT)

BUBBE GERT (IRRITABLE STOMACH)

THE FINBERGS (HAMMER TOES)

Bad traits: No Jew is shy about mentioning yours. They always came from the other side of the family. "My father-in-law had a lot of moles like you. But you get your thick ankles from the Weigerschweigers."

Tiny traits: The smallest, dumbest, pickiest, most irrelevant micro-characteristics are observed with the intensity non-Jews would accord extra nostrils.

"Babette, did you ever notice George's toe hair? Where did that come from?"

"From Uncle Charlie. Like a jungle his was."

Similarly, you are not permitted to have a trait or ailment with no history. "Asthma? Impossible. It's never been in the family."

GENES ONLY JEWS HAVE

The hotel-room-changing gene

The always-at-the-doctor gene

The talk-with-your-mouth-full gene

The do-I-look-fat-in-this gene

The make-travel-reservations-two-years-in-advance-then-*kvetch*[4]-when-the-price-drops gene

The pride-in-bodily-sounds gene, which is expressed through the following innate behaviors:

✱ To truly clear your throat, you must cough up every blob of mucus down there.

✱ It's not a real yawn if no one can hear it.

✱ When sneezing or coughing, you have enough to worry about without having to turn your head or cover your mouth.

✱ Make loud strangling and retching sounds when something goes down the wrong pipe. The more public and/or formal the venue, the louder you hock.

✱ If you don't punctuate every sentence with a burp, you're not eating enough.

✱ Liquids cannot be enjoyed without slurping noises. Especially when drinking the last of your soup out of the bowl.

---

[4] **Kvetch:** A blend of all the following: complain, grumble, bitch, moan, gripe, whine, grouse, carp.

YOUR JEWISH EMOTIONS

PERHAPS YOU'VE NOTICED THAT MOST JEWISH MEDICAL problems are created or aggravated by stress, anger, tension, and worry.

We have spent many lifetimes perfecting the emotional minefield that maintains this brain/body axis. It's your responsibility to internalize the time-tested mosaic of Jewish feelings that makes you truly one of us, within and without.

ALWAYS:	NEVER:
Agonize	Be satisfied
Resent	Think anything is fair
Be disappointed	Be a good sport
Gloat	Feel undeserving
Get even	Let go of a grudge
Suffer	Ease up
Be positive something terrible is going to happen	Acknowledge the possibility of any light at the end of the tunnel

ANATOMY OF A JEWISH COMPULSION

As a Jew, you should be perpetually preoccupied by anxieties, which—when properly watered and tended to—will bloom into a bright and robust bouquet of compulsions. Here's a freebie to get you started:

IF	THEN
Your umbrella breaks	Your hair will get wet
Your hair gets wet	You'll catch a cold
You catch a cold	You'll miss work
You miss work	You won't be promoted
Someone gets promoted over you	You'll lose face and have to quit
You can't get another job	You'll be flipping hamburgers
You get burned by hot lard	You'll be disfigured and never have a decent job again.

So . . . you'd better always have two or three extra umbrellas. Or five or six.

Leave work and go shop for them now.

iF YOU GO TO THERAPY

This will no longer be simply a matter of choosing a therapist and making an appointment. Each member of your new family will assume you're going because of them. They want this to be the case—they really, really want to be the focus of everything you (and everyone else) do. And they really, really want to help you.

Amid the hailstorm of questions you'll be asked, there's only one thing the asker really wants to know: what the doctor said about them, and how complimentary it was.

Should you be so naïve as to hint at the truth ("I feel I'm being judged" or "You leave me out of things"), be prepared for an explosion of wounded outrage. The questions that follow will serve two purposes. They will

1. Communicate their excruciating pain and disappointment at being blamed, and

2. Tug you around in a perfect circle—you will eventually agree that nothing bad happened to you, and if it did, it wasn't that person's fault.

ASKING FOR TROUBLE

THIS IS A CONCEPT UNIQUE TO JEWS. WE CAN ACTUALLY prevent bad things from happening to us by taking appropriate, if hypervigilant, precautions—dressing in layers, eating fruit hourly, avoiding store-brand tissues, and, of course, worrying (see page 55). Similarly, we guarantee misfortune by doing the opposite:

"Popping that pimple is . . .

"Don't touch that raw salmon! You're . . .

"Stop with the salt! It's . . .

"That garden tomato has
  schmutz[5] on it! You're . . .

**ASKING
FOR
TROUBLE**

BODY OAQs:

"Why am I having palpitations?"

"Is it safe to breathe this air?"

"Is that mascara, or is my eyelid drooping?"

"Why do I feel so bloated?"

"Is this ice pack sterile?"

"What am I yawning about?"

"Which is the bad one, the left arm or the right?"

---

[5] **Schmutz:** Very dirty dirt.

CHAPTER 5

Building Your New Jewish Economic Perspective

MONEY

UNDOUBTEDLY YOU ARE INTIMIDATED BY THIS ISSUE, GIVEN ALL the clichés about Jews' obsession with money. Relax—this is a fallacy. We're not obsessed with it. We've long since accepted its momentous place in our lives and simply make ourselves nauseous about everything else *while* dealing with money.

The true priorities of
Jewish life are:

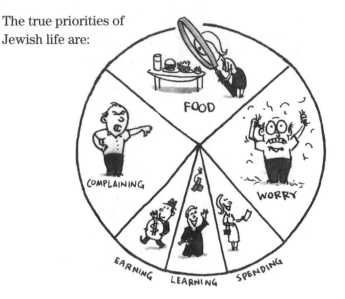

THE JOB

EWS DO NOT *WORK*. WE *HAVE A BUSINESS* OR ARE
in business or are *with a company*. Rather than being
employed by that company, we *have a position* there.

To be right for a Jewish person, a job must:

✳ Be stressful.

✳ Necessitate numerous argumentative meetings.

✳ Have ironclad deadlines that are never met.

✳ Involve tiers of people who contradict one another's instructions.

✳ Have constant technological breakdowns that are responded to
by blaming and bloviating, but not fixing.

* Teeter on an intricate pyramid of favors owed and expected.

* Include groups of subordinates crowded together who are always at each other's throats.

* Involve problems that not only can't be defined but create worse problems as you try to define them.

* Have worst-case scenarios that always come true.

* Be secured through your connections to your accountant's brother-in-law's uncle.

5 THINGS YOU CAN COUNT ON HEARING

These employment- and money-related phrases will fall around you with the steady constancy of rain:

1. "It's who you know" (intoned with a sage nod every time someone in the family gets, or fails to get, a hot job)
2. "You'll have it to fall back on" (said while pushing every student in the family toward a teaching degree, whether the kid is interested in ballet, architecture, or whaling)
3. "You get what you pay for" (said accusingly to the person responsible for buying an item, whatever the cost, that has just worn out or broken)
4. "How can you go wrong?" (demanded when you decline to buy three cases of leeks at an irresistible discount)
5. "It's an investment" (used to explain spending $895 on a blouse; it is anti-Semitic to ask, "In what?")

OCCUPATIONAL LOGISTICS AND STRATEGY

NEVER AGAIN WILL YOU GO TO WORK SMILING, IN A NICE suit and pressed shirt, and be polite and cheerful to everyone all day.

PEOPLE SKILLS

In your new work life as a Jewish person, you will have to banish such absurd concepts as *tact*, *diplomacy*, and *fair play*. These are sweet, but they don't accomplish anything.

Our Jewish repertoire of people skills has served us well for centuries. It will serve you, too, however you earn your living.

The following methodologies constitute all you'll ever need to know about dealing with people in your work, be they associates, clients, subordinates, patients, pupils, suppliers, or customers. The techniques may be used singly, or they may be alternated or combined. Of course, they all address the same objective, the only one that matters to you now that you're Jewish: getting your way.

Infuriate Them. Condescend. Belittle. Have preposterous expectations. Remember their goofs. Notice their odd habits. Hate their taste. Question their sincerity. Claim not to understand what they want from you. Wonder aloud why they're wasting your time. Pretend they're not making sense.

Love Them to Bitty-Bits. Grin. Hug. Flatter. Ask sensitive, probing, personal questions. Understand their pain. Pat their hand. Fluff their hair. Call them by adorable, original pet names. Have private jokes. Remember everything they say. Give surprises. Make confessions. Love their favorites. Send them fruit/samples/tickets/wine. E-mail them cartoons, jokes, and motivational quotes with animated puppies or dancing flowers. Text them often with sweet hellos.

Pile on Guilt. Plead. Be sorry, sheepish. Cock your head. Sniff. Squeeze their shoulder. Apologize with eloquence, humor, desperation. Hint at your poverty. Share your problems. Need their assistance. Praise their talent. Beg for their understanding. Envy their luck. Exaggerate your contribution.

Drive Them Berserk. Call them by the wrong name, a different one each time. Forget a third of what they tell you. Confuse their achievements with someone else's. Ask questions and ignore the answers. Call them repeatedly, then be unavailable when they call back. Change a date. Change your mind. Change their instructions/appointment/assignment/order/online address.

PROFESSIONAL COURTESY

If you're a professional, your new friends and relatives know you will be honored to make your service available to them at little or no charge. Here's how to handle people who won't be paying your usual fee:

✱ Make sure they have trouble getting an appointment. Feel free to change or cancel it. When they come, warn them you're pressed for time. Be distracted.

✱ Send them an itemized bill, even if they won't be paying anything. Next to each service, write "No charge."

✱ When you can get away with it, bill for part of the fee. Make a big deal on the bill about the discount. Really smack them between the eyes with what they would have paid without it.

✱ Keep saying how lucky they are to have you.

✱ Be apoplectic anytime a professional has the gall to send *you* a bill.

NETWORKING

As you begin to think like a Jewish person, you'll discover how divine it feels to be owed a favor. Networking is a fine way to build a collection of favors receivable.

Situation 1

A friend is looking for a job. You happen to overhear someone mention an opening.

Old Behavior. You pass along the lead.

New Behavior. Tell your friend you have confidential information about a once-in-a-lifetime opportunity. Make sure he understands how much trouble it was to find this out. Keep asking if he got an interview, if he had the interview, if he's heard anything yet. If he doesn't get the job, imply that he didn't pursue it correctly. If he gets it, take full credit.

Situation 2

You've decided to change careers. Furniture sales is out; screenwriting is in. Lucky for you, you knew a screenwriter thirty years ago.

Old Behavior. You do nothing. It's been thirty years.

New Behavior. Hunt the person down. Act as if you saw them yesterday. Fill them in on all the family news. Ask nothing about their family. Explain how they can help you. Should you sense any rude reluctance, make up a favor you once did for them. Who remembers after thirty years?

CONSUMERiSM

EVERY JEWISH FAMILY HAS ONE OR MORE PROFESSIONAL Consumers (PCs). These *mavens*[1] know all the best stores and services. When you buy something, they know where you could have gotten it cheaper, why it was a poor choice anyhow, and what you should have picked instead for less money.

It's easy to make errors that help PCs behave even more obnoxiously than they routinely do. Step carefully, lest you be ambushed.

Do Not:

✳ Mention in a PC's presence which bakery, butcher, hairdresser, mechanic, or piano tuner you patronize. They'll be completely familiar with its limitations and will explain in detail why it isn't nearly as good as the one they use.

✳ Change to theirs. In three months they'll be asking why you're dumb enough to keep patronizing such a terrible place.

✳ Try to top them. You can't. Your goal is simply to find a good bakery or mechanic. The PC's goal is to be able to say they have a better one.

Labels That Keep Jews from Buying Things

"Harmful if swallowed."

"Do not use near open flame."

"Hand wash only."

"Some assembly required."

---

[1] **Maven:** The most expert expert.

YOU WON'T SEE A JEWISH PERSON SPEND DOLLAR ONE AT:

* HSN
* CheapCaribbean.com
* A bake sale
* Just-A-Buck
* Academy Auto Parts
* Merry Maids
* Roy Rogers

* Krispy Kreme
* H&R Block
* Bob's Discount Furniture
* The Loan Phone
* Dollywood
* Reptile World

You PAID WAY TOO MUCH FOR THIS CAMERA. I COULD'VE GOTTEN YOU THE SAME CAMERA FOR HALF THE PRICE!

* Get trapped into recommending a place if a PC asks you to. Not only won't they like it, but they'll go on—often at length, and in front of as many people as possible—about how bad it was and how much trouble this fiasco caused them. They'll expect you to sympathize.

SPOTTING THOSE FABULOUS BUYING OPPORTUNITIES

Your new Jewish family will expect you to join them in keeping your eagle eye out for chances of a lifetime. Stay alert for hints that this occasion or product shouldn't be missed. You'll know when you see these warnings:

"Just eight tickets left at this price!"

"Going Fastttttttt!"

"Sold Out Everywhere!"

"Only 300 in stock!"

"Limited edition!"

As a non-Jew, you had the stupid idea that such statements are come-ons, probably lies, and even insulting—*who is Best Buy to scare me into spending money?* Now, though, you must understand that unavailability is a major requirement for wanting. The harder the item or experience is to get, the more precious you know it is. Otherwise, why would everyone else want it?

ECONOMIC OAQs

"Why is this iPod so cheap?"

"What am I going to do if they close Eileen Fisher?"

"Twelve-fifty for a glass of Chardonnay! How much could the bottle cost?"

"Why doesn't every country have dollars?"

CHAPTER 6

Raising Your Jewish Child

NAMiNG YOUR CHiLDREN

IN YOUR NEW JEWISH FAMILY, NAME NEGOTIATIONS WILL begin long before the first baby arrives or is even conceived. Consider yourself fortunate if your in-laws aren't hissing "Devorah!" and "Herschel!" into your ear as you walk down the aisle at your wedding. Naming your child after a relative (who must be deceased) honors that person. Thus, in the black-and-white-but-no-gray tradition of your new family's negotiations, NOT honoring the late Tanta Ruhama[1] or Zaidie Tsvi[2] is a slap in the face. Naming your child after a LIVING relative signifies wishing that person dead, which can get you arrested.

---

[1] **Tanta:** Aunt. Any aunt can be a tanta.

[2] **Zaidie:** Grandfather. This is a Jewish bear trap in itself, since only the favored grandfather gets to be called Zaidie. Picture the fallout . . .

First names fall into two categories:

Guilt: Harold, Zelda, Albert

Nouvelle: Madison, Sydney, Casey

This is also true of your new Jewish surname (which you will be known by whether you officially take it or not, regardless of your gender, because Jewish names are always dominant):

Ethnic: Garbstein, Markowitz, Mizrahi

Mayonnaised: Kane, Steen, Marks

Thus the permutations for your child's full name range from

nouvelle-nouvelle-mayonnaised: Lake Skylar Crane

to **guilt-guilt-ethnic:** Samuel Seymour Wasserfarb

with the most common choices being mixtures:

Nouvelle-guilt-mayonnaised: Riley Ora Rapp

Guilt-nouvelle-ethnic: Nathan Connor Glicktenstein

Nouvelle-nouvelle-ethnic:
Whitney Jillian Frolenkramp

or, where the family is large and the relatives vocal, longer combinations that may include an honorific name or surname from a past generation:

Nouvelle-guilt-ethnic-mayonnaised:
Mackenzie Ruth Hasselowitz Stone

Nouvelle-nouvelle-ethnic-ethnic:
Chance Jordan Kruchkow Fishkin

Guilt-nouvelle-nouvelle-ethnic:
Ina Kortni Destiny Polinsky

Guilt-nouvelle-guilt-mayonnaised:
Irwin Sean Herbert Rice

Finally, there are the combinations produced by hyphenating the parents' surnames, Jewish and Not:

Nouvelle-nouvelle-Jewish-Not:
Ryan Kirk Smolenoff-Marlow

Nouvelle-guilt-Not-Jewish:
Brooke Mildred Church-Finkfelder

THE PSYCHOLOGY OF CHILD-RAISING[3]

PERHAPS *YOU* WERE RAISED WITH DISCIPLINE AND RULES . . . where a tantrum might be ignored to teach you a lesson. Never even contemplate such criminal neglect of your Jewish child. You have to hang over your little one like a giant bat. This vigilance must carry into the child's later development, leaving no aspect of his high school and college life unscrutinized, un-listened to, un-harped on, un-nagged about.

Your child will be so grateful to realize, upon becoming a parent, who provided the emotional seedlings that flower then, all ready to nurture the next generation.

MIXED MESSAGES

You must make certain your child receives the traditional series of these throughout the growth years. How else can he or she achieve the correct *adult* psychological state, i.e., being constantly in therapy and never getting any better?

---

[3] At any library you can learn about the formal traditions of Jewish child-raising— the bris, the Hebrew lessons, the bar/bat mitzvah. The circumcision and the adulthood ceremony are actually the same event for the male child, separated by thirteen years. The only differences in the bar mitzvah are these:

• The rabbi stays longer.

• There is more food.

• No cutting is done, aside from the guests' comments about one another's outfits.

Thus, in this section we deal not with information readily available elsewhere, but with the crucial real facts that have never until now been codified—the truths without which you might tragically raise a youngster who is quiet, reasonable, and unselfish.

✱ You're the best/You'll never be good enough.

✱ Eat/Be thin.

✱ We'll take care of you/Grow up.

✱ You can't fail/You can't win.

✱ Save/Spend/Earn/Give/Buy/Keep.

✱ Don't worry/Worry.

RHETORICAL QUESTIONS

Continually repeated, these become a lifelong lullaby for the Jewish child. They establish and maintain the precarious security that is the Jewish person's birthright.

Some favorites you must not omit:

✱ "Do you want to break your neck?"

✱ "This is how you thank us?"

✱ "You're wearing that?"

✱ "For this I'm spending fifty thousand a year?"

✱ "Who am I, Donald Trump?"

✱ "Are you trying to give me a heart attack?"

KEEPiNG YOUR CHiLD'S DiET HEALTHY

SERVE LITTLE KALEIGH ANY PACKAGED FOOD WHOSE LABEL contains one or more of these terms: whole-grain, organic, vitamin A(nything), high-protein, high-fiber, low-cholesterol, recommended, cardiovascular, antioxidant, survey, doctor, dietician, or dentist. Rest assured that, even if the product is chocolate-chunk waffles or SpongeBob–shaped cereal, it tops the nutrition pyramid.

Educate other parents by gently chiding them about *their* children's eating habits. ("That mayonnaise on Ian's sandwich is poison. Haven't you ever heard of hummus?")

CHiLD-RAiSiNG TERMS YOU NEED TO KNOW

Themiddleofthenight A dangerous, otherworldly dimension that can only be escaped by sleeping ("What are you doing up? It's themiddleofthenight."). This question, repeated often and ominously, puts the finishing touch on any neuroses not already firmly embedded.

Ruin your appetite What a food will do if it's spontaneously snacked on, not served by the parent ("Don't eat that sandwich. You'll ruin your appetite.")

Grateful What your child must be continually reminded he isn't ("Who else would make you nice onions with your liver? You should be grateful.")

EDUCATION

NO SCHOOL IS EVER GOING TO COME REMOTELY CLOSE TO approaching any semblance of being the slightest bit good enough for your child. As long as you accept this fact from the start, the youngster's education will flow smoothly.

This does not, of course, release you from your obligation to monitor the entire process, from toddler years through adulthood.

You must not fail to:

1. Insist constantly and loudly that the child is bored for lack of challenge.

2. Rail against the arbitrary unfairness of standardized tests (if your child scores low) or against the ignorance of parents who consider them unfair (if your child aces them).

3. Set the teacher straight if she contacts you for any reason other than to remark on the child's brilliant intellect and radiant personality. Should she mention a "problem," rest assured there is none. Never accept any idiocy that faults the little one. You know the teacher is simply jealous because she wishes *she* had such a magnificent child. Make it clear that any issue with the child to which the teacher overreacted resulted from

✳ The unappetizing school lunch

✳ The uncomfortable temperature of the classroom

✳ Overexertion in gym class

  or

✳ The fact that the teacher knows your child is smarter than she is

4. Demand private-school quality from public school, college-level teaching from private school, graduate facilities from college, and the patently impossible from any one-to-one instruction.

college A place where children are sent after high school to get impressive decals for the family vehicles.

YOUR CHILD'S FUTURE

IT IS YOUR PARENTAL RESPONSIBILITY TO GUIDE YOUR CHILD TO a career that is, or sounds, important. Do not shrink from your vital role in this process. Your Jewish child expects to be nagged, pressured, browbeaten, and bludgeoned into a career path. Be creative in applying tactics such as threats, extortion, blackmail, and tyranny. Withhold love, money, esteem, approval, or whatever will work; you know your child best. Never back down in this crusade. Do you want your child to think you don't care?

IMPORTANT CAREER AREAS

✱ Law

✱ Medicine

ACCEPTABLE

✱ Finance

✱ Engineering

✱ Communications

✱ Publishing

iF ALL ELSE FAiLS

✱ Teaching

✱ Retailing

✱ Computer technology

✱ Social work

✱ Manufacturing

✱ Real estate

✱ Dentistry (unless you want to keep hearing,
   "He's not a real doctor, he's a dentist")

FiELDS YOU CAN FORGET ABOUT YOUR CHiLD EVER ENTERiNG

✱ The military

✱ Automotive

✱ Chiropractic

✱ Midwifery

✱ Podiatry

✱ Farming

✱ Para-anything

WHEN YOUR CHILD IS READY TO MARRY

NO ONE IN YOUR JEWISH FAMILY EXPECTS YOU TO HIDE THE fact that you hate your child's intended. Indeed, eyebrows would rise if you didn't.

Your relatives will rally around and share your disappointment. They will graciously join you in trashing the person. They will nod knowingly when, in the intended's presence, you ostentatiously button your lip and look skyward.

You can count on this unquestioning support for the best of reasons: They all know that one day, despite their best efforts, they will be in your position. They will strive as desperately as you are now to transfer their heartbreak over the loss of their child to the handiest target.

It will be your duty to help each of them just as they are helping you.

MEETING THE PROSPECTIVE IN-LAWS

This is your last chance to get their child out of your life, so use it well. If that fails, you still have much to gain from this meeting: It's never too soon to begin tipping the familial power balance. Start now, and you'll enjoy years of tactical rewards as the in-laws struggle for equality. With good early work on your part, they might not get to see the first grandchild for months.

1. Invite them onto your turf before they can summon you to theirs.

2. Present the engaged couple with tickets to some event distant enough that they won't barge in on you.

3. Find a way to put the prospective in-laws on the defensive immediately. Telling them to come an hour too late is a favorite. Their first look at you and your spouse beside your incinerated roast, bravely covering your pain, will pay off for decades.

4. Cross your fingers under the table and murmur something about your child, like "We'll have to plan the wedding around Randall's trial. It's so unfair—you'd think he'd killed someone, instead of just exposing himself." Don't worry about this getting back to your child. He knows you would never say such a thing.

5. Don't dwell on the ethics of your behavior for one tiny second. It's for a good cause. And your in-laws would have done it if they'd thought of it first.

THE WEDDING

SURELY, YOU MAY BE THINKING, THIS IS ONE AREA WHERE you don't need lessons—after all, you experienced your own wedding to a Jewish person, and your child's marriage might not be mixed.

The difference is that you did not experience the wedding from the Jewish dugout. There is much to be learned that has nothing to do with whom your child marries, Jewish or Not . . . but everything to do with *you*, the child's Jewish parents, and how this event bespeaks *your* sophistication, charm, and taste. Who do you think your child's wedding is *for*?

THE NEGOTIATIONS

As in any ethnic group, the bride's family, who are paying for the wedding, decide on the location, catering, and guest list.

In a Jewish family, *decide* is defined as *make an opening offer.*

It is simply not conceivable to a Jewish couple that they can't control their own child's wedding. You must hold this view if your child is the groom, and prepare for it if your child is the bride. Thus the best compromise one can expect between tradition and reality is that the groom's family, whether you or they, will interfere with, second-guess, badger, and outshout the bride's on every aspect of the event—in other words, negotiate.

People think a Jewish wedding is planned far in advance of the date because facilities are in demand. This is a myth. It is because months and sometimes years are needed for the rounds of necessary talks.

Topics to be negotiated include (but are by no means limited to) the following:

✱ Total number of guests

✱ Number of guests from each side

✱ Designation of cardiologist to treat coronaries resulting from battles over this issue

✱ Number of unnecessary enclosures in invitations

✱ Tent rental company (see page 140)

✱ Designation of family member to deal, in the time-honored manner, with guests who gauchely bring gift to wedding (designee must frown, reluctantly take gift, then look helplessly around for a place to put it)

✱ Photographer

✱ Ostentatiousness of photo album

✱ Choice of wedding gown. This should be hashed out between both mothers, and the bride informed of the final decision. Don't be afraid to show your displeasure as the girl tries on dresses.

✱ Band

✱ Degree of aggressiveness permitted in urging guests onto the floor for line dances

✳ Which relative(s) to block from giving a toast

✳ Hors d'oeuvre buffet

✳ Method of settling arguments among less sophisticated guests about whether this is dinner

✳ Number of entrée choices to be offered

✳ Number of substitute entrées for guests who reject all the choices

✳ Seating assignments

✳ Method of placating guests who hate where you put them

✳ Selection of seat of honor for host family's cleaning lady

✳ Designation of relative to keep loudly announcing that she's one of the family

✳ Florist

✳ Lavishness of flowers

✳ Selection of most absurd place, such as an animal shelter, to donate flowers after wedding

THE TENT

A tent must be rented for your child's wedding reception, regardless of the indoor facilities available. This ensures that you will spend as much money as possible without being deprived of the pleasure of worrying about the weather.

THE BAR

A well-stocked bar must include soda, caffeine-free soda, diet soda, club soda, and some clone of Baileys Irish Cream without the word *Irish* in the name. Anything else is optional.

THE VIENNESE TABLE

You can have a Jewish wedding without a *chuppa*[4] but not without a Viennese Table. And you must be sure to *call* it a Viennese Table. Then it won't matter what other food is served, or how little of it, because all the guests' conversations afterward will go:

"How was the wedding?"

"Wonderful. They had a Viennese Table."

THE SHOW-'EM-HOW-IT-SHOULD'VE-BEEN-DONE PARTY

(For Groom's Parents Only)

Have this party a polite interval after the wedding—say, a week and a half. Invite everyone on your side who came to the wedding, plus everyone who didn't, plus your dry cleaner, hair colorist, and decorator. Invite your son's old girlfriends, so they can see what they missed. Serve Himalayas of spectacular food. Hire a hot band. Hint that another band was lined up, but Mick had a sore throat.

Everyone will leave believing this is how the wedding would have been in the first place, but you were too polite to impose your tastes on your son's new in-laws. And are certainly too polite to admit that this is the reason for *this* party.

---

[4] **Chuppa:** The ceremonial canopy over the bride and groom, their parents, the rabbi, and any other relatives who manage to elbow their way under it.

HOW TO BE A JEWISH GRANDPARENT

IN YOUR NON-JEWISH LIFE, YOU UNDOUBTEDLY THOUGHT BEING a grandparent was a sweet, benign, nontoxic experience enjoyed by all involved.

You must forget you ever had such a ridiculous idea.

Experienced Jewish grandparents have learned the fine art of spoiling the little ones while continuing, as always, to torture their parents.

Some suggestions to get you started:

✱ Demand that your children provide a healthy diet for the grandkids by keeping sugared cereals, potato chips, ice cream, and candy out of their house. Have all these for the tots at *your* house. Explain to anyone who dares challenge this that it's your only pleasure at your age.

✱ The moment your grandchild is born, start asking the parents why he isn't reading yet.

✱ Criticize any schools or colleges the parents are considering.

✴ Keep your wise eye tuned to the grandkids' health. Make a huge fuss over any scratch, bug bite, mole, or bruise. Imply to the parents that it's their fault. Insist the child see a scratch or bruise specialist.

✴ Apparently some fools in some states have made "stalking" a crime. These people obviously have never been grandparents. Not only is stalking not objectionable for Jews—it is their duty. How are you supposed to guide and protect the little ones if you don't catch every stupid mistake made by their pathetic parents?

✴ It's your responsibility to make sure the tots are properly entertained, and their horizons widened. Frequently question the grandkids: "When are Mommy and Daddy going to take you to the ballet (. . . Epcot . . . Paris)?"

WHEN THE CHILD'S PARENTS ARE, GODFORBID, DIVORCED

These things happen. It's important to shield the little ones from any animosity. Of course, you wouldn't dream of appearing to take sides. Certainly you'd never say an unkind word to your grandchildren about the ex-spouse. But no law says you can't gasp and shake your head and mumble a Hebrew death curse when that person's name is mentioned.

CHILD-RAISING OAQS

"What's he up to?"

"How many times do I have to say it?"

"Where does she think she's going?"

"Who am I, Dr. Phil?"

"Why don't they listen?"

"Why does she have to act so *childish*?"

"How come it's always *my* fault?"

CHAPTER 7

Joining in the Customs of Your New Jewish Family

TYPES OF JEWS

NEVER MIND WHAT YOU MAY HAVE LEARNED ABOUT REFORM, Conservative, and Orthodox. These are merely brand names for the convenience of non-Jews. Your new Jewish family falls into one of the following categories. Learn the distinctions between them, as they will offer guidance on what to expect from the members of your particular clan.

The 5 Basic Types:

Vanilla Jews

Regular Jews

New Jews

Very Jewish Jews

Even More Jewish Very Jewish Jews

This last group will only associate with other Jews. Vanilla Jews will associate with anyone *but* other Jews.

New Jews are Jews who never paid attention to their religion before and now feel a need to catch up. Unobservant for years, they suddenly remember that they're Jewish and insist on reminding Vanilla Jews that they are Jewish, too. For this they use the various traditional forms of subtly communicated disapproval if one resists, such as ostentatiously saying "Happy Passover" or "Happy New Year" or "Good Shabbat," and completely ignoring Christmas and Easter, even if they used to do outdoor lights and an annual egg hunt. New Jews may have a Bar/Bat Mitzvah at age forty. Men may also have a bris (who'd make a *tsimmis*[1] over a little piece of flesh? Brides wear white at their third wedding, don't they?).

---

[1] **Tsimmis:** Literally, a meat stew with prunes in it (honest). Also, a hullabaloo.

HOW WE DiFFER

Pronouncing the Names of Jewish Holidays

Vanilla Jews: Don't mention them, but use the day off to play tennis

Regular Jews: Say them with no Hebrew accent

New Jews: Pay for lessons to learn the correct accent

Very Jewish Jews: Say them with phlegm in all the right places

Even More Jewish Very Jewish Jews: Are too busy complaining to God to pronounce anything

Observing Non-Jewish Holidays

Vanilla Jews: Celebrate Christmas, but, to be urbane, tell their kids about Hanukkah

Regular Jews: Have a "Hanukkah Bush"

New Jews: Trip over themselves ignoring all signs of Christmas

Very Jewish Jews: Light a keepsake menorah from Aunt Basha

Even More Jewish Very Jewish Jews: Life is hard—what's to celebrate?

Keeping Kosher

Vanilla Jews: Wouldn't dream of it

Regular Jews: Wince, but eat everything

New Jews: Have eight sets of dishes in case the first four encounter *treif*[2]

Very Jewish Jews: Eat coconut shrimp off paper plates

Even More Jewish Very Jewish Jews: Eat only under a rabbi's supervision

Going to Shul

Vanilla Jews: Go to *what*?

Regular Jews: Feel guilty when they're on Grand Cayman over Passover

New Jews: Walk to the farthest one in their yarmulke and tallis

Very Jewish Jews: Get *shvach* from the fast

Even More Jewish Very Jewish Jews: What *go*? We're here.

---

[2] **Treif:** Generally accepted definition: foods such as shellfish and pork that are forbidden by Jewish law. Real definition: foods New Jews used to eat and wish they still could.

EATING OUT

FOR JEWS, THE RESTAURANT EXPERIENCE IS A MICROCOSM of life, encompassing all things closest to our hearts—food, money, conversation, competition, manipulation, even worry (Will they honor our reservation? Will the soup be hot? Will they have endive foam? Will it be as good as last time?).

Restaurant dining has its own set of traditions. These are most unique. In no other aspect of Jewish life will you find conventions so different from yours.

Situation 1

You're at a restaurant for dinner. The headwaiter leads your party to a table.

Old Behavior. You sit down, order, enjoy your meal, and leave.

New Behavior. Since the first table offered is always inferior, your group must select the one you prefer and tell the headwaiter. If the original table is really poor (near the kitchen or, Godforbid, the air conditioner), you'll need time to recover from the trauma. Sit down, use the napkins, nibble on the bread, and have a nice drink of water before you move.

Situation 2

You're now settled at a table. Adjoining it—within thirty feet, say—is another party having dinner.

Old Behavior. You disregard them.

New Behavior. You must banish the misconception that other diners are uninterested in talking with you. They'd love to hear about restaurants you've been to that are better than this. To be really sociable, ask what they're eating, peer at it, comment on how it looks, and find out why they're leaving anything that's been pushed aside.

Situation 3

While you're busy talking to people three tables away, the server clears something you weren't finished with.

Old Behavior. It doesn't matter. You're full anyway.

New Behavior. Have everyone at the table wave to get the server's attention. Inform him of this travesty. See how far you can get him to go to make it up to you. Accept nothing. You're full anyway.

Situation 4

You're lunching with someone in your new family. He/she orders the roasted beets with goat cheese. That sounds good to you.

Old Behavior. You say, "I'll have the same."

New Behavior. Have the chilled lobster salad. Ordering the same dish as your companion is an affront. It implies that he/she isn't welcome to sample your meal, and that you don't wish to show your affection by doing the same.

Situation 5

You've ordered a different dish but can't quite bring yourself to eat from your companion's plate. He/she smiles warmly and hands you a forkful.

Old Behavior. You remove the food with your teeth, or transfer it to your own fork.

New Behavior. Take the fork. Smile back. Enclosing the fork in your lips, take the food. Return the fork. Women can leave behind some lipstick for an added touch of warmth. Reciprocate with your fork. Take it back.

Even assimilated non-Jews often forget the crucial last step, which is to be sure your partner sees you using your fork as intimately as he/she just did. Resist the temptation to wipe it off. Short of naming your baby after a living relative (see page 125), there's no deeper insult to a Jewish person.

Situation 6

Your group is deciding what to order. Each entrée comes with side dishes and salad.

Old Behavior. Everyone selects an entrée, picks a salad dressing, and enjoys whatever vegetables are served.

New Behavior. Your group must ask the server what vegetable and potato come with each entrée. Mix and match to get what you prefer. Have the server recite the salad dressings several times. Request one she didn't name. Find out what's in the salad, and make sure she writes down what each person wants left out. If you feel like having something like sliced tomatoes and onions instead, say so. Find out what sauce is served with each entrée. Order that, and any ingredients you might not like in the dish, on the side. If the server is ungracious about any of your instructions, complain that they should learn how to run a restaurant.

Situation 7

You've taken an elderly relative to dinner. She can't decide what to have.

Old Behavior. You make some suggestions.

New Behavior. Read her the entire menu. Don't leave out any of the helpful descriptions ("served with piping-hot fresh-baked rolls and crisp salad from our organic garden"). Read it nice and loud. Other patrons may need help deciding, too.

Situation 8

You're at your favorite restaurant, looking forward to your favorite dish, the artichoke frittata. You're told they're out of it.

Old Behavior. You order something else.

New Behavior. Use your facial expression and tone of voice to show that your night is ruined. Explain that you always order the frittata and have been looking forward to it all week. Keep whining until your tablemates (and neighboring diners) focus on your displeasure. After all, if you're being cheated out of what you want, why should anyone else have a good time?

But don't just give up. A few polite questions will determine if the evening can be saved:

"Are you sure there isn't any?"

"Are you *positively* sure?"

"Did you *look*?"

"Don't you remember I always order the artichoke frittata?"

"Can you ask the chef if he has some put away?"

"Will it still taste fresh if he does?"

"Can you have the chef make some?"

"Will it taste the same as always?"

"Will it take long? Because we're trying to catch a movie."

CHOOSING THE RESTAURANT

This is a vital negotiation that, in Jewish families, trumps which third-world country to travel to next. Expect to spend an hour or two discussing which ones you've been to, who got sick from what, and who had the best meal of their lives there. It's traditional to still be arguing over where to go when you are already seated somewhere, reading the menu.

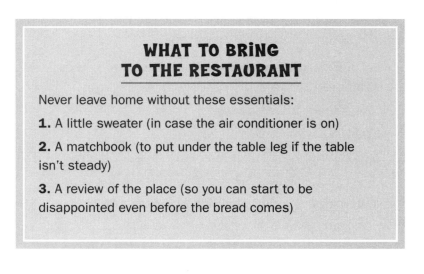

WHAT TO BRING TO THE RESTAURANT

Never leave home without these essentials:

1. A little sweater (in case the air conditioner is on)

2. A matchbook (to put under the table leg if the table isn't steady)

3. A review of the place (so you can start to be disappointed even before the bread comes)

HOW TO OVEREAT

This must be done both when dining out and when eating at your in-laws' (for extra points, do this at your own home as well). If you don't overeat, your in-laws will assume you're sick or, Godforbid, don't like the food.

✱ Burp and describe how full you are. ("I'm stuffed to the gills. Stuffed like a *kishka*").[3]

✱ Decline another serving. Be coaxed. Take more.

✱ Pick off others' plates.

✱ If dining at someone's home, snack on the leftovers while putting them into the fridge. If at a restaurant, get any leftovers wrapped up. Never eat them. Eat a gut-bursting amount of something else instead.

✱ Promise yourself you'll never do it again.

✱ Do it again.

CHICKEN MARSALA...RISOTTO...
BROCCOLI RABE...RISOTTO...
MORE CHICKEN...RISOTTO...
TIRAMISU... FRUIT...
ICE CREAM...RISOTTO...

---

[3] **Kishka:** Matzoh-meal stuffing inside a . . . trust me, that's all you want to know.

REALLY TRUE JEWiSH MOMENT

Scene: *A small snack bar inside a suburban library*

Characters: *High school girl behind counter; middle-aged Jewish woman customer*

Woman: "Do you have plain bagels?"

Counter girl: "Yes, we do."

Woman: "Do you make them here?" [Hello—it's a *library*]

Counter girl: "No, I'm sorry, we bring them in."

Woman: "They are plain?"

Counter girl: "Yes. You can see this one—nothing on it."

Woman: "Okay. Do you have butter?"

Counter girl: "Yes, we do."

Woman: "Hmmm . . . you know, I don't really want that. I really just want it plain."

Counter girl: "You can have it that way."

Woman: "Do you have any jelly?"

Counter girl: "No, we don't."

Woman: "Oh, that's too bad. You really should have jelly. Some people like it."

Counter girl: "Yes, I know. You're right. We should. Would you like the plain bagel now?"

Woman: "No, I've changed my mind. By the way, could I borrow a piece of Scotch tape?"

GUERRILLA GENEROSITY

JEWS GIVE, GIVE, GIVE, TO THE POINT OF MANIA. WE DON'T hear "no."

Let's say Rebecca is at your house and it's begun to snow. As a Gentile, you have the ridiculous idea that it's Rebecca's business how she dresses for the weather. As a Jewish person, you judge Rebecca's coat to be inadequate for her trip home and make it your mission to **give her a better one.** This exercise is performed as follows:

Inform Rebecca of your decision. Take one of your coats from the closet and hold it for her to put on. Ignore any resistance. Once you've badgered her into the coat, decide it's not heavy enough. Go back into the closet and get three more coats and make her try them on. Offer to call Aunt Gloria to bring over one of her furs.

Tell Rebecca the problem is solved for today, but does she want to catch pneumonia? Say you're going to take her shopping for a coat. Ask if she can go Sunday. If she says no, ask exasperatedly, "Well, when are we going to look at coats?"

Here's another example. You have friends over for dinner. If you're Gentile, you have no food left because you never make enough in the first place. As a Jewish person, you are up to your hips in bowls, Cool Whip containers, and Saran-wrapped bundles.

As your guests leave, gesture helplessly at the piles of food everyone always warns you not to make. Moan about spoilage and, Godforbid, waste. See how many leftovers you can bully people into taking. Inflict guilt on anyone who dares to depart empty-handed.

BUBBLE BURSTING

YOU TELL A PERSON IN YOUR NEW FAMILY SOME WONDERFUL news—about a pregnancy, a new job, a bigger house. They are excited, too. With caring interest, they ask you a question about it. After the conversation, you don't know why you feel deflated.

Here's why: Jews want everyone to be as miserable as they are. Your happiness is intolerable, and it has to be quashed. We're superb at this. Not only will you not see it coming, when it's over you won't know it happened. Count on being a member of your new family for several years before you can see what they've done to you—even in retrospect. Let's dissect the methodology:

News: You're pregnant.

Non-Jews say:	**Jews say:**
"Congratulations!"	"The doctor knows you're thirty-eight?"

News: Your little Ashley got A's in English, Math, and Science.

Non-Jews say:	**Jews say:**
"Such a smart girl!"	"What about History?"

News: Your son was just hired as an assistant at NBC-TV.

Non-Jews say:	**Jews say:**
"What an achievement!"	"They're going to promote him when?"

News: Your husband won a spot in the lottery to run the New York Marathon.

Non-Jews say:	Jews say:
"Wonderful!"	"What about his meniscus?"

News: Your daughter just got her real estate license.

Non-Jews say:	Jews say:
"I'm so happy for her!"	"She feels the market will go up?"

News: You just made an appointment for a lip augmentation.

Non-Jews say:	Jews say:
"You'll love it."	"They can avoid the trout pout?"

REALLY TRUE JEWISH MOMENT

Scene: An on-campus buffet in a tent, celebrating a medical school graduation

Cast: Graduates and their families all speaking simultaneously

"The lines are so long!"

"Where are the knives?"

"What's this on the lettuce? Alan, *you* taste it."

"You have mustard on your lip. No, the other side. No, you're missing it. Here, let me."

"Does your chair tip backward?"

"Someone has to sit with Yitzak."

"Where did you find the California rolls?"

"Napkins! We need more napkins!"

"Are these seats taken?" (Asked without waiting for an answer, while six people squeeze into a space for three)

MAKING INAPPROPRIATE JOKES

CENTURIES AGO IN THE DIASPORA, WHEN YECH HELPED himself to more than his share of matzo at the supper table, his brother Yoch would crack everyone up by saying, "Nu, Yech, that tapeworm's gonna crawl outta your *tochas* any time now!"

It's customary for us to select the most embarrassing settings to offer up a disgusting thought or ridicule a family member. Shout your comment as loudly as possible; you don't want anyone in another room to miss it.

Here are the peak times to let fly a howler:

✷ A man takes off his shirt ("Do poodles run in your family?")

✷ A relative is in the bathroom a while ("Earth calling Gertrude. Whadja, fall in?")

✷ A tall woman has on a fur coat ("What did they skin— Sasquatch?")

✷ A 30ish woman wears braids ("*Hello*, Heidi!")

✷ Something on the dinner table looks different ("Who made this potato salad? It looks like it's already been digested.")

EXPLAINING WHY NOT

WE JEWS NEVER ANSWER A QUESTION WITH "YES" OR "NO." We view any inquiry as an opportunity to fling our personal business at a captive audience. Here's how:

Situation 1: You're asked if you'd like a pastrami sandwich. Your response: "Pastrami? No, no. Too salty. I use so little salt, you know. They're watching my blood pressure very carefully. My doctor is upset because I won't give it up entirely, but you have to live . . ."

Situation 2: You're invited to sit down on someone's sofa. Your response: "I have to avoid upholstered furniture. It's terrible for my back. In fact, I had to order all new oak chairs for my living room. They clash with the walnut dining room set, but my doctor insisted I get them immediately. . . ."

Situation 3: Friends ask you to join them for dinner at a restaurant ten minutes from your home. You have young children. Your response: "No, we can't go that far away. Tessa just had her first nightmare. It's hard to get her to sleep anyway, and if she wakes up and we're not there to make her steamed soy milk . . . "

The asker, having asked, has no choice but to listen until you're done explaining why not. Ignore any checking of watches, glances at doors, or sobbing. They *asked*.

12 THINGS YOU WON'T SEE IN A JEWISH DRIVEWAY

1. A dune buggy
2. A bicycle built for two
3. A U-Haul truck
4. An air horn
5. Turtle Wax
6. A jack
7. A Kia
8. A dirt bike
9. A trailer hitch
10. An IROC
11. Any car without college stickers
12. A "Welcome to the Sapersteins'" sign

GIVING DIRECTIONS

AS YOU'VE LEARNED, JEWS ADORE ANY OPPORTUNITY TO speak authoritatively. And how much better does it get than telling people how to find *you*? There is a tradition here. When it becomes your turn, follow this example:

Say Aunt-in-law Shirley invites you over for coffee. You request directions. Have plenty of paper to take them down, because you are about to hear not a verbal map, but a travelogue.

Shirley will say, "Take Smith Road to Jones Avenue. There's a gas station on the right where you'll turn, I think Mobil, but maybe Hess. No, it's Mobil. After you turn, you'll pass a Baskin-Robbins on the left, and a dry cleaner on the right, next to PetSmart. Keep going till you come to the fork at the library. Wait, it's an Exxon station on the corner of Jones. Bear left, but not too far left or you'll be on Clock Street. You don't want Clock, you want Cardinal. Cardinal *Avenue*, not Cardinal Terrace, that's a whole other direction. As soon as you see Len's Liquors, put on your blinker . . ."

Jews offer these unnecessary landmarks to reassure you—as you pass them, you'll know you're going the right way. But you'll get lost anyhow, and Aunt Shirley will take that very personally and quiz you on where exactly you made your mistake. All the guests will then discuss how they get to Shirley's from *their* houses—including the traffic conditions on those routes at any given time of day—and will tell you what to do next time.

If you manage to arrive on time after following Shirley's directions, you must fulfill the driver's role by wiping your brow and saying, "You didn't tell me there was a hair salon, so I thought I was going wrong."

COMPLAINING

THERE IS NO SUCH THING AS A MOMENTARY COMPLAINT. You need to make sure your points are thoroughly understood.

Say you order hot wings in a restaurant. They're served without celery and bleu cheese dressing. Of course, you're thunderstruck. You say so. The server is sorry you're disappointed. Whatever she says, you say:

"Well, it's traditional."

"It provides a contrast to the hot wings."

"Every restaurant has it."

"I can't imagine why you don't."

Every time the server appears after that, repeat the abovementioned phrases. Then say them all to the hostess on your way out.

Bother Like nausea, bother is a state of being in which you will now often find yourself. Bothering one another and being bothered are ethnic pastimes. People bother us; then we bother others by complaining about how we've been bothered. In turn, we worry that we've bothered the people we complained to. And *that* bothers us.

ARRIVING/STAYING/NOT STAYING/ LEAVING/NOT LEAVING

ANOTHER HALLOWED TRADITION IS STOPPING BY PEOPLE'S houses just for a second. This can be done for several reasons, among them to

✱ Borrow something (a DVD, an E-ZPass, the forty-cup coffee maker you always cadge so you won't have to buy one).

✱ Make some excuse ("I thought I left my umbrella yesterday") to show off a new coat, handbag, or bracelet ("What, this? I've had it since we went to Kuala Lumpur").

✱ Pretend you don't know they're having a party you weren't invited to:

Stand in the person's house with your coat on, leaving the front door open. Have your partner wait outside with the motor running. Every five minutes, insist that you're only staying a second. (Twenty minutes is the minimum for only staying a second.)

A family member inside must be nominated to keep going out and asking the partner incredulously why they don't want to come in.

Others inside have to keep asking each other, "Doesn't he want to come in? Why doesn't he want to come in?"

Once you leave, your non-visit will be the topic of discussion for the entire evening.

USiNG TECHNOLOGY iN YOUR NEW FAMiLY

JUST BECAUSE TECHNOLOGY HAS GIVEN US MANY NEW ways to be in touch, and to contact others without actually interrupting them (see Bother, page 165), this does not diminish our need to communicate in traditional ways. When Jews want to communicate, it has to be *NOW*.

Here's how to proceed: E-mail the person. Text them to make sure they got your e-mail. Call them to make sure they got your text.

Similarly, never trust your GPS alone to get you where you're going. What does *it* know? Compare the route it gives you with what MapQuest says. Then call Uncle Ira. If he disagrees with the GPS, pester other relatives, until you get a *minyan*.[4]

E-MAiLiNG

This is the best innovation for Jews since the French manicure. How wonderful that we can now bloviate across the world in an instant!

Let your thoughts and feelings flow in e-mails. Don't bother turning off Caps Lock or correcting your typing—abbreviated messages are standard now. What idiot wouldn't understand "FGT 4 YIULU ATTEN PLOTTO"?

Besides, the sooner you finish, the sooner you can send another one.

---

[4] **Minyan:** A quorum. For Even More Jewish Very Jewish Jews, a minyan is ten men in a synagogue. For confused drivers, five relatives texting will do.

TEXTING

The mother of all interrupters, the text message is a delight to send. Just picture the recipient's pocket erupting in a vibrating rat-a-tat during a staff meeting or synagogue tea—it brings a glow. Never again need you doubt that you have their attention, and everyone else's.

So what if you're only texting to say your mosquito bite itches? It's the spectacle that counts. With everyone jumping up and pestering the textee to answer, you'll never have to wait for a response.

Another great pleasure is **texting with subtext.** The zenith of annoyingly amorphous grenades like the single-word salvo (see page 26), your text screen can annihilate any healthy adult with messages like "wher r u?????" and "ok have fun. may not b here when u get back but we'll c."

YOUR RINGTONE

Before you were Jewish, you were probably in the habit of **not bothering anyone.** You'd never have selected an offensive cell phone ringtone.

We Jews feel that since we're the ones who have to listen to our ringtone all the time, we can have what we want. If a nice loud Run-DMC song or a parrot squawking is fun for us, fine. Why are all these ringtones available if we're not supposed to pick the ones we like?

PANiCKiNG

ONE OF OUR MOST HOLY TRADITIONS IS PANICKING. CERTAIN stimuli cause us to widen our eyes, breathe rapidly, gesture, stutter, hyperventilate, and call other Jews. We do not speak here of space aliens or suicide bombers, but of matters particularly threatening to Jews. We love to assume the worst possible outcomes for whatever we're doing. For example, non-Jews simply go to a movie. Jews are certain that

✳ We'll be late.

✳ We'll have to park far away in a dangerous dark corner.

✳ We'll have to sit too close to the screen or too far from it.

✳ Everyone around us will be talking or chewing or wearing tall hats.

✳ The movie we want to see will be sold out.

✳ The only one not sold out will be full of bloody kung fu.

CONCEPTS THAT CAUSE JEWS TO PANIC

* Rush hour
* Port-o-san
* Vermin
* No credit cards
* Road trip
* VA hospital
* Salad bar
* Crop dusting

* Walk-in clinic
* Campground
* Bobbing for apples
* Contaminant
* Vinyl siding
* Secondhand
* Online degree
* Uninsured

CROP DUSTERS! RUN FOR YOUR LIVES!

FUNERALS

YOU'VE PROBABLY ALREADY LEARNED THAT JEWISH FUNERALS must take place within twenty-four hours of the passing. When inquiring about the reason for this urgency, you may have been told some nonsense about the absence of embalming.

That is not why.

The real reason is that there is no drama in *planning* a funeral. A longer time line would preclude the customary theatrics and stress. This way everyone has to cancel whatever they're doing, call their workplaces, postpone their golf games, miss class, and not get their roots done.

> **Dear Ms. Jewish,**
> Why must Jews wear hats to funerals?
>
> **Dear Ms. Not,**
> To hide the fact that they're not crying as devotedly as the family requires.

Mourners may compete over the importance of the canceled event ("Norma had to reschedule a tax audit"; "Well, *Roger* was scheduled to perform the president's prostate surgery"). You also get to tell all persons you notify that there has been a death in the family, collect condolences, choke back sobs, and exchange favorite funeral platitudes, including "He's in a better place" and "You don't have to come to the service" (which means you do have to).

DEATH SHARiNG

Formerly, when learning of a passing, you expressed your sympathy and that was the end of it. Among Jews, this is merely the jumping-off point for a spirited conversation.

Following the commiseration, your role is to wait expectantly and interestedly for the details of the demise. Remember that in your new family, no one dies of "natural causes." Death is always someone's fault:

✳ "No wonder his appendix ruptured. He never sat up straight."

✳ "What did she expect, *potchki*-ing [5] around in the Mekong Delta?"

✳ "Food poisoning from a picnic, he got. If God wanted you eating in the woods, He would have put you in a tree with a banana in your hand."

---

[5] **Potchki:** To play (especially where no sane person should).

After properly assigning blame, you will go on to describe other passings you've experienced or know of. A back-and-forth will ensue, as you and your conversation partner compare increasingly horrendous expirations ("Herb's aunt Malka was hit by a cab"; "My cousin Esther fell off Mount Rushmore").

At the end, you will exchange one or more clichés:

"Well, what are you gonna do?"

"Death is a part of life."

"It's all up to the man upstairs."

Bumper Stickers You'll Have to Scrape off Your Car

Baby on Board

This Car Climbed Mt. Washington

Life's a Bitch. Then You Die.

Jesus Loves You

I Brake for Big Boobs

Easy Does It

My Kid Can Beat Up Your Honor Student

Mechanics Do It with Grease

12 WAYS TO UPSET A JEWISH PERSON

1. Pick up a bowl of perfectly good food and say, "I'm throwing this out."

2. Begin a sentence, "This is probably nothing . . ."

3. Go to kiss them after kissing the dog.

4. Bleed.

5. Wear a used dress from a thrift shop. Don't wash it first.

6. Look at their baby and say, "He's so cute, but—oh, never mind."

7. Have in your kitchen several packages of whatever salmonella-ridden product is currently being recalled.

8. Buy something and drop the receipt on the floor. Leave it there.

9. Get rained on.

10. Drive your new car through mud and don't wash it.

11. Fish. With live bait.

12. Go to the pool without sunblock, a long-sleeved shirt, and a hat big enough to shade your face and those of everyone around you.

CHAPTER 8

Readiness Test

THINK YOU'VE LEARNED ENOUGH TO FUNCTION IN YOUR NEW Jewish family? Take this quiz to find out.

1. Which of the following is a Jewish medical myth?

    a. Cholesterol is one of the five food groups.

    b. "Bad back" is a medical term.

    c. Orthopedists earn as much as ophthalmologists.

2. What's the proper thing to do after asking someone a question?

    a. Sit back

    b. Make eye contact

    c. Interrupt the answer

3. You won't catch two Jews

　　a. Getting lap dances

　　b. Doing Patrón shots

　　c. Whispering in a duck blind

4. Which of the following is the best advice about dieting?

　　a. Eat only grapefruit.

　　b. Eat only sushi.

　　c. Eat only with very thin people you hate.

5. Which five words does a Jewish person never hear?

　　a. Hail, Mary, full of grace

　　b. Father, son, and holy ghost

　　c. Do you wanna supersize that?

6. A Jewish man will never

　　a. Skip a prostate exam

　　b. Be uncircumcised

　　c. Pee outdoors

7. Jews spend their vacations

　　a. Sightseeing

　　b. Sunbathing

　　c. Discussing where they spent their last vacation and where they'll spend the next

8. If there's a hairdresser in your immediate family, you are

    a. Up on the newest styles

    b. Entitled to free haircuts

    c. Not Jewish

9. If you're Jewish, "wilderness" means

    a. No running water

    b. No electricity

    c. No hot-and-sour soup

10. On which island will you never find a Jewish person?

    a. Aruba

    b. Martinique

    c. Rikers

11. A Jewish skydiver is

    a. Careful

    b. Insured

    c. An apparition

12. When all three of your children graduate from medical school, this is called

    a. A proud moment

    b. A time to celebrate

    c. A Jewish trifecta

13. "Safe sex" means

   a. You're not ovulating

   b. You've been to the *mikvah*[1]

   c. He's a bond trader

14. No Jewish person in history has ever been known to

   a. Deface a synagogue

   b. Work at Hooters

   c. Remove the back of a TV set

15. A Jewish person would hate to be placed in

   a. Danger

   b. San Quentin

   c. An Econo Lodge

16. The word *anal* is derived from

   a. The noun *anus*

   b. The adverb *anxiously*

   c. The Hebrew adjective *analechhh*, meaning "exactly like a Jewish person"

17. You'll never find a Jewish person on

   a. Methamphetamines

   b. Adult FriendFinder

   c. *The Bachelorette*

---

[1] **Mikvah:** A ritual immersion women take in a public shared bath that somehow makes us clean enough for Jewish men.

18. A guaranteed sign of impending death is

   a. Fluid in the lungs

   b. Internal bleeding

   c. A phone call after 10:00 P.M.

19. Jews are afraid they'll get

   a. Colds

   b. Headaches

   c. Every ailment someone else has

20. It's perfectly appropriate to ask a patient in the hospital,

   a. Are you feeling better?

   b. Can I bring you anything?

   c. How could you do this to me?

21. Jews only whisper when

   a. Having a migraine

   b. Buying condoms

   c. Discussing other Jews in the room

22. Jews love to collect

   a. Hummels

   b. Stamps

   c. Injustices

23. Which is most likely to give you an ulcer?

    a. Going to fast-food restaurants

    b. Going to Indian restaurants

    c. Going to restaurants that don't take reservations

24. What is the major function of the colon?

    a. To digest food

    b. To process gas

    c. To cost you $2,000 for a horrible test that says it's fine

25. When your Jewish stomach is full, you are

    a. Satisfied

    b. Ready for coffee

    c. Only halfway through dinner

26. Jews are never

    a. Airheads

    b. Buttheads

    c. Parrotheads

27. Clinical depression serves the following function:

    a. To rid your brain of toxins

    b. To protect your nervous system

    c. To keep Jews from enjoying anything too much

28. You'll never catch a Jewish person selling

    a. Crack

    b. Amway

    c. Short

29. Jews flirt with

    a. audacity

    b. blondes

    c. *treif*

30. You won't see a Jewish person

    a. Running scared

    b. Running amok

    c. Running with the bulls at Pamplona

Scoring: Take 1 point for each **a** answer, 2 for each **b,** 3 for each **c.**

76 to 90: Mazel tov! You know a lot about Jews. Either you've studied your new family carefully, out of your desire for true closeness plus your respect for their traditions, or you're from Florida. They'll adore you.

60 to 75: You're not quite there yet, but don't panic. Just remember to do everything louder, longer, and with a lot more butter than you used to.

30 to 59: Sorry. Better go back to the beginning and start again. Or consider leaving town and buying a Quiznos franchise.

REALLY TRUE JEWISH MOMENT

Scene: *A car full of Jews has just entered a parking garage. The following chorus ensues:*

"The sign says 'no unauthorized parking.' What does that mean?"

"Don't back in. Nobody else is backed in."

"You're crooked."

"Not so close to the wall. We won't be able to get into the trunk."

"We don't *need* to get into the trunk."

"Well, in case."

"Isn't this area just for the valets?"

"We're going to get towed."